C000000696

Walk!

Menorca

by

David & Ros Brawn

DISCOVERY WALKING GUIDES LTD

Walk! Menorca
First Edition 2005

Copyright © 2005

Published by
Discovery Walking Guides Ltd
10 Tennyson Close, Northampton NN5 7HJ,
England

Maps
Maps are adapted from **Menorca Tour & Trail
Map** (ISBN 1-904946-03-8) published by
Discovery Walking Guides Ltd

Photographs
All photographs in this book were taken by the
authors, Ros & David Brawn

Front Cover Photographs

Cala Trebalúger
on Walk 23

Trepucó on Walk 4

On route to Binimel-
Lá, Walk 38

Descending to
Cales Coves,
Walk 29

ISBN 1-904946-02-X

Text and photographs* © David & Ros Brawn

Walk! Menorca

CONTENTS

THE WALKS

David & Ros Brawn

David and Ros have lived and worked in England, Papua New Guinea and the Seychelles before settling for a number of years in Tenerife. David's first published books were accountancy texts.

David and Ros have been walking and writing for Discovery Walking Guides since it began, researching guides for most of the Canary Islands, the Balearic Islands, Malta, Gozo, Madeira, the Alpujarras and the Sierra de Aracena. More recently they have surveyed and mapped a number of these regions using satellite navigation equipment combined with cartographic software.

Considering themselves as semi-permanent travellers, they divide their non-research time between Spain and Northampton, England.

David is a member of the British Cartographic Society.

David & Ros are the authors of a number of publications to various destinations including:

Tour & Trail Maps
Tour & Trail Super-Durable Maps
Walkers' Maps
Drive! Maps
34/35 Walks Guidebooks
Walk! Guidebooks
Portable Navigator Files (PNFs) on CD

David is also the author of:

GPS The Easy Way

MENORCA - THE LIVING MUSEUM

The sheer quantity of prehistoric buildings and remains in Menorca is breathtaking, in fact, nowhere else in the world boasts so many in such a contained area. It's also a pleasant surprise to find that many of them are easy to reach by car or on foot. More remains are being found and liberated from concealing cloaks of vegetation, some sites being carefully restored using the fallen stones in the vicinity; others are left in the natural state in which they were found. Major excavations are under way in the **Cap de Cavalleria** area where a Roman town is gradually being uncovered (Walks 35 & 36).

Menorca has never had many trees, so its almost inexhaustible supply of stone was always the obvious building material of choice. One of the main reasons why so many settlements survive from prehistoric times is that the local limestone is relatively soft and easy to cut and work, yet once exposed to sun and light it becomes hard and develops strength and durability.

Some of the more important and accessible sites provide information boards and car parking areas, and one or two now have opening hours and charge a modest entry fee - many others, though, seem eerily untouched by recent centuries or the authorities.

There's plenty of history from less distant eras. Menorca's coastline boasts many watchtowers dating from the 16th to the 19th centuries, and the remains of other military establishments, also dating from the 16th century and up until the Spanish Civil War. **Maó** and **Ciutadella** and several other towns are steeped in history. Most of our walks on Menorca have some historical interest; in fact, it's difficult to avoid! If you're particularly interested in walks with historical content, try these:

Walk N°		
7	Torre d'en Penyat	Defence tower, dates from Napoleonic times
6	Fort Marlborough	18th century Fortress
4	Trepucó Settlement	Menorca's biggest *taula*, a majestic *talaiot*, and a *hypostyle* chamber
5	Trebalúger	Large *talaiot* within a walled enclosure
12	Torrelló	A *talaiot*, and a sixth century mosaic church floor, Fornas de Torrelló
13	Talatí de Dalt	Prehistoric settlement
	Rafal Rubí Vell	Two *navetas*
35	Unnamed settlement	Prehistoric *poblat* and *naveta*
	Torre de Sa Nitja	Watchtower
36	Cap de Cavalleria	Gun emplacements
39	Mola de Fornells	Abandoned barracks
16	Torre Blanca	Prehistoric *poblat*
25	Torre d'en Galmés	Large prehistoric settlement (*talaiots*, *taulas*, *hypostyle* buildings and a water storage and filtration system carved from rock)

25	Lluc al Lari	Military camp
26	Son Bou Basilica	Remains of early Christian Romanesque church
30	Santa Agueda	Roman road, and site of Moorish Castle
29	Cales Coves	*Necropolis* caves
33	Son Mercer	*Naveta*
32	Santa Ponça	Quarry
28	Santa Mónica	*Talaiot*

Hypostyle Chambers

Stone pillars, broader at the top than at the bottom are the key feature of these low buildings. Roofed over with large flattish slabs of stone, they were often built over a depression or excavation so that the 'room' inside is partly underground. Two good examples of Hypostyle Chambers can be found at **Torre d'en Galmés** (Walk 25) and **Trepucó** (Walk 4).

Hypostle chamber

Navetas

Navetas are often situated a few hundred metres from the main settlements, as they were used as burial chambers. The name 'naveta' translates as 'boat', and these stone-built structures do resemble up-turned boats. Some have two levels, such as the restored Naveta as **Es Tudons**, easily reached from the main Me-1 road into Ciutadella. Another good example can be visited at **Rafal Rubí.** (Walk 13)

Taulas

Experts argue about the possible purpose of the Taulas; some believe they are altars, while others think they may represent bulls' heads, as these animals were revered in prehistoric times. Whatever the explanation, the Taula is an impressive massive stone slab, made to stand upright in a bed of rock, and with a 'table-top' of flat stone slab balanced on top, and often with a supporting smaller slab angled against it.

They can be seen in a number of the prehistoric village settlement sites, and are partly enclosed by a mini Stonehenge-like arrangement of smaller standing stones. Two easily reached examples can be seen at **Torralba** (Walk 22) and **Talatí de Dalt** (Walk 13), although there are many others dotted around Menorca.

Taula at Torre Blanca

Talaiots

These roughly cylindrical stone mounds, usually around 7-10m high, seem to have been an integral part of most ancient settlements.

Trebalúger Talaiot

The majority are solid structures, while a few have a doorway and inner room. As with Taulas, their precise use or meaning is open to debate. One theory is that the most important man of the village might have lived in - or even on - the Talaiot, perhaps with a further structure on top, although if these existed they are long gone.

Talaiots are commonly found, two of which can be examined at **Torrelló** (Walk 12) and at **Trebalúger** (Walk 5).

Necropolis Caves

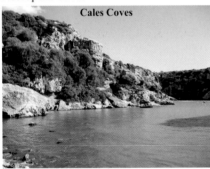
Cales Coves

Burial chambers dating back to Talaiotic times were hollowed out from natural fissures in the limestone into large caves which were used as a necropolis, which also became holy places of pilgrimage. The most spectacular examples in the Balearics, and in the most dramatic setting, are at **Cales Coves** (Walk 29)

FLORA & FAUNA

Much of Menorca's countryside is characterised by gently rolling hills and dales, green meadows and thickets of trees. Many fields are divided by pale stone walls which provide habitats for many varieties of plants and insects. The wilder areas of the island include wetlands, rugged cliffs and a coastline blessed with bays and beaches. The clean air and lack of pollution, along with the lack of major developments and industry, ensure that plants and wildlife thrive.

Trees, shrubs and plants

Common trees that you will see on a number of our walks include olive (*Olea europea*), holm oak (*Quercus ilex*), strawberry tree (*Arbutus unedo*), Aleppo pine (*Pinus halepensis*), mastic tree (*Pistacia lenticus*).

Some of the many shrubs and plants commonly found on our routes include tree heather (*erica arborea*), myrtle (*Myrtus communis*), gladioli (*Gladiolus communis*), Italian sainfoin (*Hedysarum coronarium*), French lavender (*Lavandula stoechas*), rock rose (*cistus* - various species), sarsparilla (*smilax aspera*), wild rose (*Rosa sempervirens*)

Capparis spinosa (caper), common on Menorca

Also look out for members of the lily family, asphodels and orchids, as well as a wide variety of more humble wild flowers and grasses.

Birds

Menorca is home to many species of resident birds, and also plays host to migrating and over wintering varieties. You will usually see some bird life in all areas of Menorca, but areas of particular interest to bird watchers are:

S'Albufera	(Walk 14)
Aveagua	(Walk 17)
Galdana Gorge	(Walk 20)
Son Bou	(Walk 26)

Just a few of the commonly seen birds: Cory's Shearwater, Mediterranean Shag, Egyptian Vulture, Booted Eagle, Stone Curlew, Rock Dove, Scops Owl, Hoopoe, Tekla Lark, Fan-tailed Warbler, Raven, Sardinian Warbler.

Wildlife

You'll see lizards sunbathing on rocks or hear them scuttling into the undergrowth. There are three varieties on Menorca;
Lilford's wall lizard with a distinctive rather stubby tail shaped something like a turnip, the Moroccan wall lizard with an olive skin, and the Italian wall lizard, a bright olive green with black stripes.

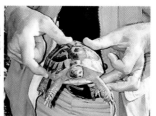

Wild tortoises trundle determinedly around the island, and are more likely to be spotted on walks passing through wooded areas, and on country strolls offering shade and cover.

You'll see many varieties of butterflies, bees, beetles and snails, especially in farming areas where uncultivated fields are a riot of wild flowers and grasses.

Islands, by their very nature of being islands, are prone to individualistic tendencies, which observed from the outside might be seen to be rather quirky. Menorca is no exception, and in its land ownership might even set a new style of quirkiness. The island might look like Devon transported to the mediterannean - well, its country areas at least; but the creation of this delightful landscape results from the land owners' unusual approaches to managing the land.

Travel around rural Menorca, and you are transported to the land of Sleeping Beauty. Grand magisterial country houses look out over lands that haven't been farmed for decades, the land reverting to nature while waiting for the magic kiss of development. It wasn't always like this; once the land bustled with agricultural activity as workers sowed and reaped, herded and sheared, on the working farms that produced the money to build grand country houses. Gentlemen landowners were gentlemen farmers, while others were gentlemen stone quarriers (see Walk 32 where the quarry was the wealth that created the magnificent **Santa Ponça** country house).

Villas of Convenience; Menorca's Second Homes

In the early twentieth century it was all very well making your fortune from farming, or quarrying, but that didn't always satisfy the gentlemens' family who craved a brighter life than that available on a country estate. The solution was to build 'Villas of Convenience', miniature villas sited alongside the main trade road (now the ME-1 main road) between the twin capitals of **Maó** and **Ciutadella**. Here, members of the family could decamp with a couple of servants to observe the passing trade, a very bustling existence compared to life on the country estate.

Classic examples of these Villas of Convenience second homes can be seen alongside the ME-1 east of **Alaior** in the form of **Villa Taunus**, **Macarena** and **Casa Segunda**, but for the best examples, take the old main road into **Alaior** and look for the excellently preserved mini-villas set above the south of the old road. The most unusually sited of these early twentieth century second homes is at **Cales Coves** (Walk 29), set as a retreat above the beautiful inlet.

Plotlands and Land Plots; the New Farming

Menorca's abandoned farmland is a recent phenomena. Fifty years ago, you would still find a bustling agricultural economy. Agriculture, and quarrying, was the main income of the grand country estates until the second half of the twentieth century. As trade and professions developed, many gentlemen farmers found that it was much easier to simply be a gentleman, rather than a farmer, organising the estate and its workforce with your income subject to what the trade would pay for your product.

Landowners owned the land, most of the island being owned by the country houses. How much easier to rent out the land to people in the trade, who thought they could make a profit from farming. Affluent people from the towns wanted a stake in the countryside and, more importantly, were prepared to pay for it. Create a dirt road access, and you could sell off agricultural 'plotlands', these smallholder plotlands proving popular with town-living weekend farmers. Classic examples of these plotlands semi-agricultural developments are seen to the north of **Binissaida** (Walks 7, 10 & 11) and north of the **Ferreries - Migjorn Gran** road (Walk 33).

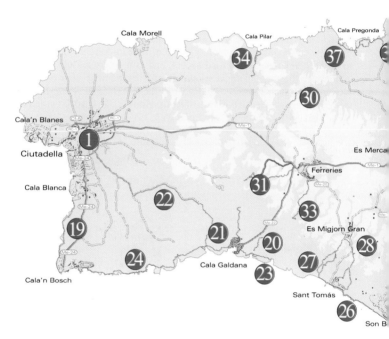

Cala Morell

Cala Pilar

Cala Pregonda

34

37

30

Cala'n Blanes

Ciutadella

1

Es Merca

Cala Blanca

Me-1

Ferreries

Me-20

31

22

33

Es Migjorn Gran

21

28

19

20

24

27

Cala Galdana

23

Cala'n Bosch

Sant Tomás

26

Son B

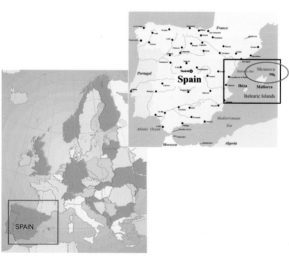

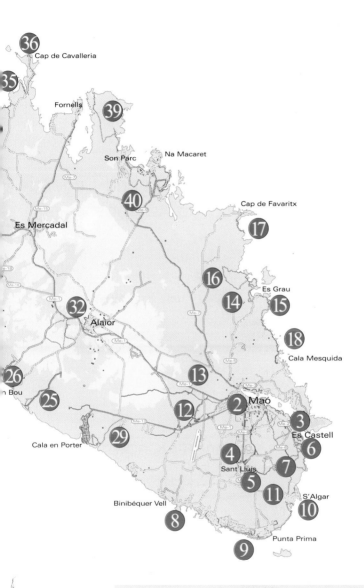

Cap de Cavalleria

Fornells

Son Parc

Na Macaret

Cap de Favaritx

Es Mercadal

Es Grau

Alaior

Cala Mesquida

Maó

Es Castell

Cala en Porter

Sant Lluís

S'Algar

Binibéquer Vell

Punta Prima

Map adapted from

Menorca Tour & Trail Super-Durable Map

Published 2005 by Discovery Walking Guides Ltd Northampton
NN5 7HJ England.
ISBN 1-904946-03-8
© Copyright David & Ros Brawn 2005

The map sections used in this book have been adapted from **Menorca Tour & Trail Super-Durable Map** (ISBN 1-904946-03) published by Discovery Walking Guides Ltd. In the interests of clarity, not all waypoints referred to in the walk descriptions are shown in the map sections.

Menorca Tour & Trail Super-Durable Map is a 1:40,000 full colour map. For more information on DWG publications, write to:

DWG Ltd, 10 Tennyson Close, Northampton NN5 7HJ, England,
or visit:

www.walking.demon.co.uk   www.dwgwalking.co.uk

Menorca Tour & Trail Legend-Legende

ALTITUDE, HÖHE, ALTITUD, ALTITUDE

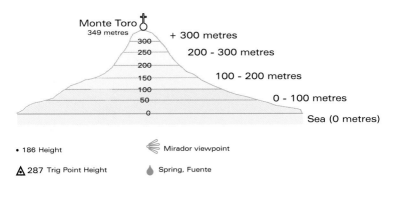

Monte Toro
349 metres

+ 300 metres
300
250   200 - 300 metres
200
150   100 - 200 metres
100
50   0 - 100 metres
0
Sea (0 metres)

• 186 Height

△ 287 Trig Point Height

🐚 Mirador viewpoint

💧 Spring, Fuente

ROADS, STRAßE, CARRETERA, ROUTE

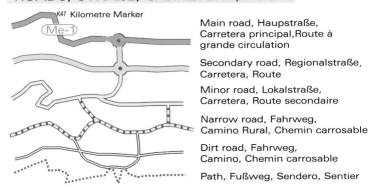

K47 Kilometre Marker

Me-1

Main road, Haupstraße, Carretera principal, Route à grande circulation

Secondary road, Regionalstraße, Carretera, Route

Minor road, Lokalstraße, Carretera, Route secondaire

Narrow road, Fahrweg, Camino Rural, Chemin carrosable

Dirt road, Fahrweg, Camino, Chemin carrosable

Path, Fußweg, Sendero, Sentier

🏠 Large House, Casa Major   ⊟ House, Casa      Urban area

🗼 Tower, Torre   🗼 Lighthouse, Faro   ⚲ Chapel, Ermita   ⛪ Church Iglesia

P Parking   ⌨ Bar/Rest   🏨 Hotel   ⛽ Petrol   ⛩ Picnic area, Zona Recreativa

⚽ Sports Ground, Campo Deportivo   ⛺ Camping   ⊞ Cemetery, Cementario

🌬 Wind Turbine, Eólica   🏚 Historical Site, Ruinas   🏚 Ruin/Barn/Uninhabited

🐢 Our sightings of tortoises

Walking Routes, Wanderweg, Sendero, Chemin.

Walk! Menorca Route (Red) 17

GPS Waypoint
see Waypoint Lists

8

our rating for effort/exertion:-
1 very easy   **2** easy   **3** average
4 energetic   **5** strenuous

 approximate **time** to complete a walk (compare your times against ours early in a walk) - does not include stopping time

 approximate walking **distance** in kilometres

 approximate **ascents/descents** in metres (N = negligible)

 circular route

 linear route

risk of **vertigo**

refreshments (may be at start or end of a route only)

Walk descriptions include:

- timing in minutes, shown as (40M)
- compass directions, shown as (NW)
- heights in metres, shown as (1355m)
- GPS waypoints, shown as (Wp.3)

Notes on the text

Place names are shown in **bold text**, except where we refer to a written sign, when any place names are enclosed in single quotation marks.

Spanish words are shown in *italics*, and if also in *purple*, will be included in the glossary (P.129).

Menorca's rolling landscape gives the impression that navigation should be easy. On the ground it is a different matter, with high bushes and walls obscuring the view, and a lack of local landmarks to focus on. While most walking routes are easy to follow with a good route description, some present quite a challenge, Walk 18, Cala Mesquida - Es Grau, posing the toughest navigational test. Knowing exactly where you are is a great confidence builder when exploring new landscapes. GPS waypoints give you pin-point navigational accuracy, allowing you to enjoy the walking route free from worries about wayfinding.

All The GPS Waypoints quoted in **Walk! Menorca** were recorded during the research of the walking routes, and are subject to the general considerations as to the accuracy of GPS units in the location concerned. It is virtually impossible to reproduce the exact GPS Waypoint co-ordinates in practice when walking a route, and 5-10 metres is an acceptable standard of accuracy when you have '3D navigation' (four or more satellites in view) on Menorca. Only in extreme situations, such a the cliff path descent on Walk 29, Cales Coves Circular, are you likely to experience poor GPS reception.

GPS Waypoint co-ordinates are quoted for the WGS84 datum, used to provide grid references on **Menorca Tour & Trail Super-Durable Map**, in degrees and minutes of Latitude and Longitude. To input the Waypoints into your GPS we suggest that you:

- switch on your GPS and select 'simulator' mode, 'demo' mode on some units,

- check that your GPS is set to the WGS84 datum (its default datum) and the ' position format' '°.mm.mmm',

- input the GPS Waypoints into a 'GPS route' with the same number as the walking route number; then when you call up the 'GPS route' on Menorca there should be no confusion as to which walking route it refers,

- repeat the inputting of routes until you have covered all the routes you plan to walk, or until you have used up the memory capacity of your GPS; even the most basic of GPS units will store up to 20 GPS routes of up to 50 waypoints for each route, and you can always re-programme your GPS while on Menorca,

- turn off your GPS. When you turn the GPS back on it should return to its normal navigation mode.

Personal Navigator Files are GPS track and waypoint files that cover all the destinations in our current range of Walk! guidebooks, including **Walk! Menorca**. Both track and waypoint files for walking routes can be downloaded direct to your GPS unit from the PNFs CD using a PC. Your GPS navigation information is transferred in seconds - so much easier than manually inputting waypoints.

GPS Waypoints are provided as an additional navigation aid to complement the detailed walk descriptions in Walk! Menorca. Knowing exactly where you are in relation to our detailed walk description is a great confidence booster when exploring these new landscapes. GPS Waypoints are provided for all key navigational points on all walking routes; never again should you find yourself wondering whether you are on the right path or not.

Note that GPS Waypoints complement the detailed walking route descriptions, and are not intended for use as an alternative to the route description.

Confused by GPS?

If you are confused by talk of GPS, but are interested in how this modern navigational aid could enhance your walking enjoyment then simply seek out a copy of GPS The Easy Way. Thousands have benefitted from the straight forward explanation of GPS navigation and graded exercises to bring GPS novices up to advanced GPS user status.

"A compass points north."
but
"A GPS tells you where you are, where you've been, and can show you where you want to go."

GPS The Easy Way is available from bookshops, outdoors shops, over the internet, and post free from:

Discovery Walking Guides Ltd.
10 Tennyson Close
Northampton NN5 7HJ

More information on GPS The Easy Way and Personal Navigator Files CD is available on our websites:

www.walking.demon.co.uk

www.dwgwalking.co.uk

WALKING EQUIPMENT

Menorca's gentle rolling landscapes belie the fact that walking conditions on the island can be quite harsh. Trails can be on uneven and broken rock, bushes are scratchy much of the time, and you can be a long way from a refreshment stop. Adding in the Mediterranean climate means that it will pay to be a well prepared walker. At the risk of upsetting some sensibilities, here is what we have used during our research on Menorca.

BACKPACK

A 25 litre day pack should easily cope with all the equipment you think you will need for a day's walking. A design with plenty of outside pockets to give easy access to frequently used items, such as ½ litre water bottles, is a good starting point. Well padded straps will spread the load and a waist strap will stop the pack moving about on the more adventurous routes. A ventilated back panel will help clear sweat on hot days and tough routes; a design with a stand-off frame is best for ventilation and worth the small increase in weight. Do spend time adjusting the straps, so that you get the most comfortable fit.

As an alternative to traditional backpack designs, you might find the cyclists' packs produced by Nikko, and similar companies, a good compromise of stand-off frame, capacity, pockets and weight.

FOOTWEAR

While there are many comfortable paths on the island suitable for trainers, some of the walking is on hard rock, often uneven, where you will benefit from tougher footwear. Whether you choose boots, shoes or sandals, they must be up to the task. My (David) current favourites are a pair of Bestard Race K shoes from their factory shop on Mallorca. Worn with thick mountain socks, these boots have done everything I have asked of them though they probably seem a bit over the top for an island like Menorca. Ros has walked the routes in a mixture of Merrell and Cats sandals. One consequence of wearing low-cut footwear is that we do get a lot of scratches from the bushes, so you might consider long socks, trousers or even gaiters as part of your walking equipment.

Whichever footwear you choose, do make sure that you have covered plenty of kilometres in them before coming to Menorca.

SUN PROTECTION

Always carry a comfortable sun hat, also useful should it rain. Choose a design that gives you plenty of shade, is comfortable to wear, and stays on your head in windy conditions. You will be spending several hours a day outdoors and sunburnt ears (and neck) are both painful and embarrassing. Sunglasses and high-factor sun cream are highly recommended.

Our own choice is for Rohan Legionnaire style caps and wrap round sunglasses.

WATER & FOOD

Always carry as much water as you think you might drink. A couple of ½ litre bottles, a few pence each from local shops, is the minimum, and add another couple of litres for longer or more strenuous routes. Even on shorter routes, we would advise that you carry some survival rations. While some routes are well equipped with *tipico* bars, survival rations of chocolate bars and the like can provide welcome comfort.

MEDICAL KIT

Antiseptic wipes, antiseptic cream, plasters and bandage are supplemented by lip salve, which can seem like a life saver in hot dry conditions. Also include tweezers, which you'll soon appreciate if you catch a splinter, and a whistle to attract attention if you get into difficulties.

NAVIGATION

Do not compromise - buy the best guide book and the best map, and carry them with you. A compass is useful to orientate yourself at the start of a route and for general directions, but a GPS unit is far more useful - see our section on 'Using GPS for Walking Navigation on Menorca' on page 19.

CLOTHING

Choose loose comfortable clothing and add a lightweight waterproof jacket to your back pack; the Balearics are famous for sunshine, but we have always had at least one day's rain during our research trips to the island.

OTHER EQUIPMENT

You won't want to be carrying excess weight during your walking. Digital cameras usually weigh far less than their film equivalents, and a monocular is half the weight of a pair of binoculars. Secateurs might seem an unusual choice of walking equipment, but they will come in useful on overgrown routes at the start of the season and are so much easier than trying to snap back intrusive branches. A mobile phone, and money (refreshments, taxis, public telephones, drinks machines etc.) are also recommended.

If you arrive by bus from the beach resorts south of the city, the ride terminates at **Plaça Esplanada**. Buses from other areas finish at the bus station on **Carrer Barcelona**. Car drivers will find parking tricky although there is a chance of spaces at **Plaça d'es Born**; otherwise, be prepared to park on the outskirts of the town.

The walk proper begins at **Plaça Esplanada**, so those arriving at the bus station or parking on the edge of town need to make their way to this point. To avoid getting lost, follow the broad **Avingudas** which are built on the lines of the old city walls. Heading west will soon bring you to **Plaça Esplanda**.

We cross the road with the bus stops on it on the north of the square and bear right into **Plaça d'es Born** marked by its towering **Obelisk** commemorating those who lost their lives in the Turkish invasion of 1558 which flattened most of the town. Occupying the north-west corner of the square is the **Ajuntament** with its stone arches and stately palms. Step inside to examine the Gothic reception areas and memorabilia including portraits of past dignitaries. This is a 'working' town hall so you can go inside during office hours and from 18.00 to 20.00 hours on weekdays. Turning right as we leave the town hall, we take the steps leading up to the viewpoint of **Bastió d'es Governador** (17th century) tower to overlook the harbour.

Back in **Plaça d'es Born**, we cross to its east side, dominated by **Palau Torresaura** with the family coat-of-arms carved over its main archway. On its right stands **Palau Salort** on the corner of **Carrer Major del Born**, open for viewing in summer (10.00-14.00). We continue clockwise round the square passing **Palau Vivó** to face one of the few churches to survive the Turkish destruction, the Gothic **Església de Sant Francesc**, with baroque additions. We walk along **Carrer de la Purissima** by the side of the church and take the second left, **Carrer de Beat Ramon Llull**, following it to its T-junction with **Carrer de Sant Joan Baptista**. We turn left onto the street, and then first right into **Carrer del Santissim**.

We are entering one of the interesting shopping streets of this old central area; for example, the antique and furniture restoration shop on the right is housed in the elegant **Can Saura** (17th century), and we pass leather, silk and craft shops as well as **Palau Martorell**, the austere residence of the Marques de Albranca, on our left towards the top of the street. Keeping on this street as it angles around the **Seminari** which houses the **Diocesan Museum**, brings us onto **Castell Rupit** and on into **Plaça de la Libertad**. We can take a few minutes to look around the fruit, vegetable and fish market (**Mercat**) in the square.

Leaving the square on the **Carrer de l'Hospital de Santa Magdalena** at its north-west corner, we then take the first left (**Carrer del Socors**) which leads us to **Calle del Seminari**, a shopper's paradise of small specialist shops. On the corner as we enter the street stands **Església del Socors** on the left, and a

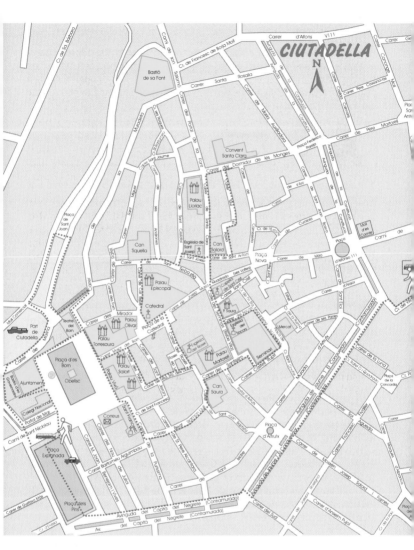

bank occupies what was **Palau Saura** on the right. Turning right along the street, passing the little baroque chapel of **Capella de Sant Crist** (1667) with its octagonal dome, on our right. Continuing ahead, we meet and cross **Carrer de Josep Maria Quadrado** to the street opposite which angles slightly right, **Carrer de Santa Clara**. We walk along past **Església de Sant Josep** on the left and **Can Salord** on the right before passing the austere lines of **Palau Lloriac** on the left. Taking the next right onto **Carrer del Dormidor de les Monges**, we walk along to take a look at **Convent Santa Clara** on the north side of the road, its original buildings dating back to 1287 but rebuilt after the Turkish invasion, and restored again in the twentieth century. Doubling back for a few metres, we go left down **Carrer Qui No Passa** to its T-junction with **Carrer de Sant Antoni** where we turn right around the corner of **Can Salord** and walk the few metres to meet **Carrer de Santa Clara** and cross straight over to take the short street almost opposite, **Carrer Sant Josep** with the church on its corner. A left at the next junction brings us to **Carrer de Sant Sebastiá.**

Turning right takes us west along **Carrer de sant Sebastiá** to take the next turning left onto **Carrer de Cal Bisbe**. The building on our left is the **Palau Episcopal**, the Bishop's residence which shares a site with the **Catedral** itself, dedicated to St. Mary. A mosque once stood here, and although a Christian church occupied this area from 1362, it was destroyed by the Turks in 1558 and gradually rebuilt. The newest addition to the building is the west wing, on the corner as we enter **Plaça de la Catedral** with the **Tourist Information Office** opposite. On the other side of this corner stands **Palau Olivar**, yet another grand home owned by one of the elite families, the Olives.

We leave the square on **Carrer de Roser** opposite the older south door of the **Catedral**. This street is the location of more small specialist shops, and also the eye-catchingly ornate baroque **Església del Roser** about half way along it on the left, now used as an exhibition venue. At the end of the street we turn right onto **Carrer de Notra Senora dels Dolors**, keeping on it as it bends right and becomes **Carrer des Palau** before it meets the T-junction with **Carrer Major del Born** with the **Palau Torresaura** facing us. We go left here and are now back in **Plaça des Born**.

Heading right to the north side of the square, we pass the **Teatro del Born** theatre as we enter **Carrer de sa Muradeta**, looking out for steps down to the harbour on our left after the street angles left and right. After strolling around the harbour area, we find another flight of steps off the **Carrer de Marina** behind the town hall (**Ajuntament**) which take us back up to street level onto **Camí de Sant Nicolau** which leads us back to our starting point in **Plaça Esplanada**.

Maó city makes the ideal stroll, taking in its noble buildings and its magnificent and historic harbour. It's easy walking with plenty of potential refreshment stops to tempt you, so regard our time estimate as flexible.

Access by bus: to **Maó** bus station then walk the few metres to **Plaça de s'Esplanada**.

Access by car: follow the car parking signs into central **Maó** from the ring road to the underground pay car park.

We begin in **Plaça de s'Esplanada** to stroll across the square to cut through on the short street on its north-east side and on to **Carrer Sa Rovellada de Dalt** where we can find the **Tourist Information Office** almost opposite, well woth calling in to pick up information about the town and the island.

Plaça de s'Esplanada

Turning right as we leave the office, we take the **Carrer d'es Negres** to the right, and on reaching the T-junction with **Carrer s'Arraval**, head right.

We take the next street on our left, **Carrer Sant Antoni**, first taking a look at the building on its corner. This is now the **Sala de Cultura**, a venue for shows, exhibitions and concerts although it was once the church of Sant Antoni, Menorca's patron saint. Following the **Carrer Sant Antoni**, we take the first street on our left, **Carrer Sant Jaume**, turning first right leading into the **Plaça d'es Monestir** with **Església de Sant Francesc** facing us. This church with its ornate baroque façade, thought to have been built in the 17th to 18th centuries, used to be the home of the monks of Saint Francis. To the left of the church stands the **Museu de Menorca**, a museum which has housed a Franciscan convent, high school, public library and orphanage during its previous lives.

Leaving the square by **Carrer de Isabel 11** opposite the church, we stroll along one of the streets favoured since the 18th century by Menorca's elite. House N°2 was the rectory, while N°s 6-8, **Casa de Pons y Soler** houses an art collection. About half way along the street at N°9 is the **Gober Militar**, easily spotted by the sentry posted outside this residence of Menorca's Military Governor. This building was once the home of King Alfonso 111, and the British Governor resided here during Britain's governership of Menorca in the 18th century, when Menorca was part of the British Empire. The upper

storeys are often the most attractive features of these noble buildings, and you can spot the use of sash windows - an eighteenth century British import and rarely found anywhere else outside the United Kingdom. Look out for houses numbers 58, 60 and 62 whose plaques detail the names and achievements of those who once lived there.

Towards the end of the street the **Ayuntament** (town hall) marks our arrival at **Plaça de la Constitució**. The town hall, on the north edge of the square, dates back as far as 1613 although it was rebuilt in 1788. Look for the English clock set in its wall (donated by Sir Richard Kane, first British Governor of Menorca) to locate the entrance and step inside to see portraits and the coat of arms from Fort St. Philip. On the east side of the square is the **Church of Santa María**, while the impressive old **Guard House** stands on the west side. Turning right (W) after the guard house onto **Carrer d'Església** takes us past the post office and into **Plaça Bastió**. Going north (N) through the square takes us to the last remains of the ancient medieval town walls, the **Arc de Sant Roc**, which still retains two towers and intact battlements. Continuing ahead along Carrer de Rector Mort takes us back towards **Carrer Isabel 11** which we cross, still heading north, turning right at the T-junction onto **Costa des General** which takes us down to the harbour.

After enjoying a stroll along the water's edge, and probably giving in to the temptation of a refreshment stop, we take the pedestrian route back up to the town through **Parc Rochina** which emerges at **Plaça de la Conquista**. The square houses the **Casa Cultural** (formerly Casa Mercadal) dating from 1761 and was the home of one of Menorca's noblest families, constructed on the foundations of a castle. Now a cultural centre, it is home the public library, archives and an art gallery. The square is also occupied by **Església Santa María** and a statue of King Alfonso 111 as a young man. From the square we take a small detour to the right along **Pont d'es Castell** from where there are excellent views of **Maó** harbour.

We retrace our steps into **Plaça de la Conquista** and turn left to leave the square on its southern side. Going straight ahead (SW) soon brings us into **Plaça Espanya**, passing the fish market (built in 1927) on our left. Continuing in the same direction leads to a large Carmelite church and its cloisters, built between 1750 and 1835 within the imposing **Plaça del Carme**. The convent of the Carmelite nuns, built in 1751, is the massive baroque building which immediately catches the attention, no longer occupied by nuns but housing shops in the basement and ground floors and a cultural centre on the upper floor. At the south-east corner of this area we turn left onto **Plaça Miranda** and leave it at its front right corner to join **Costa de Levant**, looking for the steps which make for our short cut down to the harbour, where we go right (E).

The harbour road takes us around the neck of the inlet and as we turn south, we see the **Club Maritim** ahead. Taking the steps climbing up away from the water after the club, we then cross over the **Passeig Maritim** and turn next left onto **Avinguda Font de L'Eau**, then taking the second right onto **Carrer del Carme** which skirts the edge of the college and sports fields. We go first left onto **Carrer Sant Joan**, continuing to the T-junction with **Camí d'es Castell** where we turn right. After passing the ornate nineteenth century **Consell Insular** (N°28) we take the next left, passing the neo-classical **Casa Olivar** with its Italianate painted ceilings (now a furniture shop) at the next T-junction where we go left and then first right onto **Ramon i Cajal**. Once past the **Club Deportivo Alcázar**, look for the path on the right which takes us across the pleasant **Parc d'es Fregenal**, emerging onto **Costa d'en Ga**. Turning left takes us to the **Teatro Principal** (1825), where taking the street opposite, **Carrer de Sant Jordi**, leads us up to the crossroads with **Carrer de Cos de Gracía**. We go straight across here, passing the **Hospital Municipal** on our left, then turning right at the T-junction to find ourselves back in **Plaça de s'Esplanada**. But before collecting the car or waiting for a bus, take a look at the barracks (**Quarter de s'Esplanada**) dating back to the British occupation, and the Monument to the dead of Spain's Civil War (**Monumento**) which stands in the square.

3 FROM TOWN TO TOWN: MAÓ - ES CASTELL

Our first out of town route has a little bit of everything; ancient city, deep water harbour, small settlement and a hidden entrance into the countryside. If you are staying in **Es Castell** this walk (in reverse) is a very pleasant alternative to bussing into **Maó**. GPS reception is poor/nil in **Maó** and **Es Castell's** narrow streets, while the stroll around the harbour hardly justifies the need for satellite navigation so track and waypoints are provided for the country section of the route only.

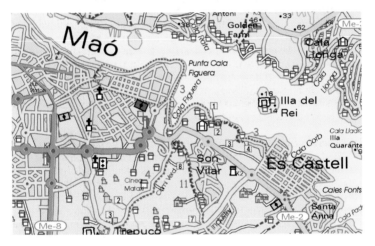

Our starting point is in the bustling **Plaça de S'Esplanada** of **Maó** (0M), just below the bus station and very busy on market days. From the north-east corner of the *plaça* we take the **Carrer de ses Moreres**, a one-way street lined with small shops. Staying on this main street, we make slow progress (in hiking terms) through the crowds of tourists until we come to a T-junction with **Carrer Bastió Costa Deia**. Here we leave the traffic behind but not the crowds, to go straight over the junction onto the pedestrianised **Carrer de Hannover**. We head steeply downhill between the shops and crowds, towards the **Santa María** church. The narrow street opens out into the small **Plaça Colón** with its statues and drinking taps, before dropping down beside the impressive church. As we come to the end of the street (6M) we have a choice of routes; our longer waterfront stroll, or a short cut through the narrow streets of the old town.

Short Cut

At the end of **Carrer de Hannover** we go right and follow the traffic past the fish market (*Mercado Pescado*) and climb up to the **Plaça de Carmé**. Crossing over and keeping on the left hand side brings us to the **Carrer de Carmé**. This narrow street is lined by old but rather featureless houses, and we stroll down to meet a modern road at a junction that has a bank (*caixa*) on its corner. From the junction (17M) we can see the main road roundabout, a hundred metres away on our right. We go straight over the road onto **Passeig Maritim**. As the *passeig* swings left we come to a path on our right leading through a gap in the concrete wall. Through the wall, the path branches, one section going left to a small park while we go down the steep concrete steps on the right. The concrete stair takes us down past an electricity substation to emerge onto **Carrer de Costa Correa**. Turning left, we go down the steep street to the waterfront junction where we rejoin our main route (21M).

The Main Route
Emerging from the **Carrer de Hannover**, we go straight over the road to a wide stairway. Flights of stairs take us down through this public park, crossing the zigzagging road to bring us onto the harbour by the modern sculptures (9M). Across the road again, we are at the departure dock for boat excursions. We turn right at the waterfront to stroll past the port administration offices for a couple of minutes before our route comes up alongside the main road. It is easy walking on this part of the walk even though there are still plenty of tourists, as we pass **La Minerva** floating bar/restaurant and the small boats moored along the quayside. We come along to **Maó**'s 'mermaid' statue and head towards the **Il Porto** restaurant. Gradually the tourist crowds thin out as we swing right to follow the inlet of **Cala Figuera** away from the main harbour. More easy strolling takes us past the **Club Maritimo** and an impressive staired ascent up to the **Passeig Maritim** before meeting our short-cut route at **Restaurant Jagarro** (27M).

We go left onto the narrow road - don't walk through the boat repair yard as it is a dead end; immediately the nature of our route changes, and there is now just the odd local boat and few tourists as we walk along beneath the limestone ridge to the head of **Cala Figuera**. At the head of the inlet the road goes inland while we continue on a narrow lane to pass in front of the CHL depot. We swing around the head of the inlet, looking back over the calm waters to our earlier route, as we stroll past **Apartamentos Cala Figuera**. On our right is a limestone ridge, and we come to the end of the inlet and swing right, the nature of the walk abruptly changing once again, this time from limestone to the terraced buildings of this small settlement which faces the harbour. Continuing along the lane we pass **Bistro 44**, **Hostal Miramar** and finally **Restaurant Miramar**.

As we approach the end of the settlement the lane narrows where a building stands on the seaward side of our route. Ahead we see the lane curve left to finish in a slipway by a dilapidated building. Undeterred by this sight, we continue on towards two mature trees hiding an electricity substation. The house numbers count down to Nº15, where we leave the tarmac to climb a flight of concrete stairs (Wp.1 42M).

The concrete stairs at Wp.1

We swing left on the stairs to continue up past a green-doored house and **Las Gavinas**, complete with its own coat of arms. A few metres on, the concrete path finishes at **Casa Burnet** and we continue on a small path that climbs through a stone wall.

We come into a small meadow which our faint trail crosses and then climbs up a stone slope to a junction (Wp.2). From the junction, we take the main trail which follows the line of a low stone wall above the harbour's cliffs. After the mostly urban nature of our walk so far, we now find ourselves in an abundant sea of wild flowers which push in on our route as we walk along the top of the cliffs alongside an old stone wall, breached occasionally to give *mirador* viewing points over the harbour. On our right, the stone-walled fields have been taken over by verdant wild plants, as our trail cuts through the walls to come to an isolated cove opposite **Illa del Rei**, once used as an isolation hospital. Here an old trail drops steeply down to our left; our original route but now blocked by the yellow house across the steep valley from us. Keeping to the main trail we come inland to a junction (Wp.3) where we go left to meet a tarmac road at its turning circle just beyond the yellow house (Wp.4 53M).

The tarmac road, **Carrer Agamenon**, takes us through this quiet, but heavily parked, area, swinging right past some new houses and **Hotel Agamenon** before coming up to a road junction. Turning left, we go gently downhill past streets off to our right until we reach **Carrer Bon-Air** just before a steep lane goes down to our left. We turn onto **Carrer Bon-Air** and follow it to its end at a T-junction overlooking **Cala Corb**. We go left and come to a gap in the concrete wall where a steep concrete stair takes us down to sea level. Walking up to the head of the inlet, we pass **Bar Picatapas** which makes a pleasant refreshment stop. We ignore the road out of the inlet and take a narrow concrete stair by the sign **Moli de Cala Corb** which climbs steeply to the cliff top where we emerge into a little square at the end of **Carrer de Cales Fonts**. Just a few metres along its route **Carrer de Cales Fonts** opens out into **Plaça de S'Esplanada**, a former parade ground for the old army barracks which faces the square. There are bars and cafés in the *plaça*, but for more stylish refreshment you should go one street inland to **Carrer Gran**. This is **Es Castell**'s main shopping, eating and drinking street offering a good choice of hostelries during peak tourist season.

For the bus back to **Maó**, continue up to the main road where the terminus is opposite the football ground beside the roundabout.

Usually we avoid road routes, keeping to country trails whenever possible, but here we make an exception with a choice of two routes on quiet lanes from **Maó** to the archaeological site at **Trepucó**. The site at **Trepucó** and its *taula* and *talaiot* are impressive and memorable, but there are no refreshments, either at the site or in the hamlet. This would be reason enough for us to search for a country route to a hostelry, and if you add a narrow country lane running through beautiful countryside, you have the second stage of our route. Unfortunately the last kilometre has to be on a 'main' road into **Sant Lluís**, but don't let this dissuade you as the road is more 'main' in name than in traffic flow.

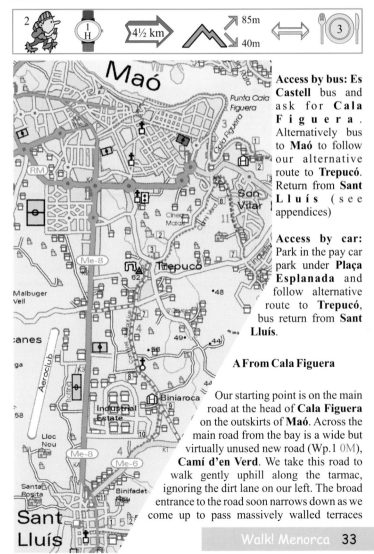

Access by bus: Es Castell bus and ask for **Cala Figuera**. Alternatively bus to **Maó** to follow our alternative route to **Trepucó**. Return from **Sant Lluís** (see appendices)

Access by car: Park in the pay car park under **Plaça Esplanada** and follow alternative route to **Trepucó**, bus return from **Sant Lluís**.

A From Cala Figuera

Our starting point is on the main road at the head of **Cala Figuera** on the outskirts of **Maó**. Across the main road from the bay is a wide but virtually unused new road (Wp.1 0M), **Camí d'en Verd**. We take this road to walk gently uphill along the tarmac, ignoring the dirt lane on our left. The broad entrance to the road soon narrows down as we come up to pass massively walled terraces which line the canyon on our right. Limestone caves border the left side of our road as we continue to climb steadily up out of the canyon.

The road passes **Cinea Maxtania** and levels out to a more gentle gradient, for us to stroll along past the entrance to **Equimar Equestrian Centre** (Wp.2 14M), and abandoned fields and huts. Past a traffic sign for a junction, we pass a trail off on our left, and in one hundred metres come to the 'main road' (Wp.3 17M) and the 'Talaiot Trepucó sign'.

Across the main road, we walk along a narrow lane (Wp.4) which twists round a farmhouse between high walls. We come to a limestone-cobbled trail on our right which we follow to cover the last few metres into the site (Wp.5 22M) - look out for the large cave at the start of this little lane.

Trepucó

Trepucó is a large walled site with standing stones as well as the *talaiot*. From the walls, we can see what appears to be a smaller *talaiot* or *naveta* across a cornfield, though not accessible from this site. You soon have to become used to the lack of catering and bus access at archaeological sites, a significant reason for us to head off for **Sant Lluís** on quiet country lanes.

B Alternative Route from Plaça Esplanada

Leaving **Plaça Esplanada** on **Carrer de Moreres** in a few metres we turn right onto **Carrer Cos de Garcia** to stroll out to the ring road. Carefully crossing the dual carriageway, we go straight over onto a lane signed 'Talaiot de Trepucó'. We walk up the lane, passing another sign before we reach a junction to follow another **Talaiot de Trepucó** sign along **Camí d'en Verd** to the limestone lane which takes us past a large ground-level cave and into the archaeological site.

Trepucó to Sant Lluís

Walking back down the rough limestone lane from the archaeological site at **Trepucó**, we come onto the narrow tarmac lane (Wp.6 0M). We follow the traffic sign and turn right to stroll along the narrow lane past the *talaiot* and come to a group of traditional farmhouses where the lane opens out. A few metres on, passing the terrace which includes the pink **Villa Rosenado**, we come to a main lane.

Going straight over the cross-roads (Wp.7 7M), the lane here quite wide and named **Camí Vell de Sant Lluís**, as we walk along to pass an old house on our left and a pair of newer terraced houses on our right. The lane narrows as we come past an unusual new building and an electricity sub-station, to go gently downhill. Dry stone walls press in on the lane as we walk along to a monument topped with a cross (Wp.8 19M), though unfortunately, the monument is dwarfed by a huge warehouse behind the opposite wall.

On reaching the monument we find that its drinking fountain and any inscriptions have been weathered away, but we do get good views from its steps, over the countryside to the forts and prison near the entrance to **Maó** harbour. Our lane swings left for us to stroll gently downhill between fallow fields, the lane opening out as we come to a cluster of country houses; the impressive **Biniaroca Hotel Rural** set amongst them. Past the houses, we come to a junction (Wp.9 27M) and again follow the traffic instructions by taking the lane to the right. We pass a large villa on our left as the lane narrows, and we pass a breeze-block walled smallholding just before our route wriggles its way onto the main road (Wp.10 33M).

Sant Lluís is in sight as we walk in single file down the 'main' ME-6 road to drop down into a shallow valley. We come up a gentle gradient to meet the first houses of this small town. The road goes through S-bends (Menorcan traffic calming? Take care on this section.) between traditional cottages, to bring us up to a main road junction (Wp.11 45M), opposite the BP petrol station. We carefully cross over the main road and take the little street, **Bisbe Sever**, to come to a public square.

Across the square and to the windmill brings us onto the main street of **Sant Lluís**, **Carrer Sant Lluís**. We turn left to see the welcome sight of red and green drinks signs, indicating hostelries. Walking down the street, we come to the first of these, **Bar/Restaurant La Rueda**, a bustling establishment, popular with the locals and with air conditioning - most welcome on a hot summer's day.

Are we up for an easy country stroll taking in an enchanting little settlement and finishing at an historic site with elevated views over the surrounding settlements? Of course we are, so here is a route for us strollers; free of intrusive shrubbery and with easy route finding. Unfortunately there are no refreshments, and the only way to make it into a circular route is to return along the ME-6 road which is not an appealing prospect.

Access by bus: to **Sant Lluís**.

Access by car: follow the ME-8 to **Sant Lluís** where it bypasses the main town area and either park on the ME-8 or turn east to park on the side streets at the start of our route.

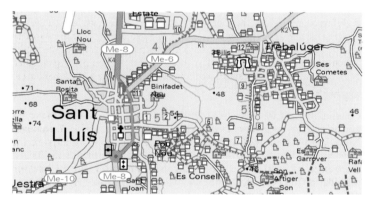

Our start point (Wp.1 0M) is on the ME-8 where a 'correos' sign points east along the **Carrer de Sant Antoni**; there are no refreshments en-route, so you might look in at the eclectic French style cafe on the opposite side of the main road for croissants before starting out.

When another 'correos' sign points left we keep straight on to pass the **Club S'Algar** warehouse on our right to come into the countryside. Traditional houses line the southern side of the little lane as we come to the **Camí d'es Pou Nou** (Wp.2,) by house N°4-91D.

Ceramic name plaque on the route

Taking the **Camí des Pou Nou**, a tiny tarmac lane running between farm buildings and houses and opposite **Es Vinyot,** another tiny lane goes left. The renovated village houses along the lane are much sought after so transforming the relatively poor farming community of **Pou Nou** into an affluent expat community who are 'worth a bob or two'. Coming to a junction (Wp.3 8M) we follow the **Camí d'es Pou Nou** to the left as it wriggles through the jumble of houses to take the **Camí de Pou Nou de Baix** (Wp.4) at a junction.

Pou Nou well

We stroll down to the well (Wp.5 14M) that gives the settlement its name, after which the houses thin out as we come up past a little lane to come up to the continuation of the main lane from **Sant Lluís** (Wp.6 17M). Turning right we stroll along past **Ca Na Julia** (left) and **Villa Estrellita** (right).

The low stone walls along the lane allow views of the countryside (unlike some walled routes) to arrive at a junction (Wp.7 23M) shortly before the **Es Rafalets** country house; the **Camí de Trebalúger** leaving the lane on the left. Leaving the tarmac we follow the *camí*'s stone laid track (N) gently downhill and then gently uphill as it narrows to a trail (Wp.8) for a short section until it widens again when a track goes off to our left. Now we start passing the gated entrances of the outlying houses, our route now named **Camí Vell**, to come to the edge of **Trebalúger** at a junction of tracks (Wp.9,).

Continuing ahead we cross a square traffic island, the **Camí Vell** now with a tarmac surface, to come onto the village 'main' street beside **Trebalúger Nova** (Wp.10) where the **Carrer de Sa Torre** goes right. Going left, we come to a junction by the rubbish and recycling bins, signed left to 'Talaoit Trebalúger' (Wp.11) where we follow the **Camí d'es Talaiot** between dilapidated farm buildings to the olive-wood gate entrance (Wp.12 38M) to the *talaiot* site. The stone-mound *talaiot* occupies a slight high point, and climbing (carefully) up to its top layer rewards us with panoramic views over the surrounding countryside.

Unfortunately, there is little more to discover at the site, so after a picnic we either retrace our outward route (recommended), or if you insist on a circular route walk along the ME-6 (not recommended), back to **Sant Lluís**.

6 GUARDS, GUARDS!

Fort de Marlborough has been reinstated as a tourist attraction and they've built a new car park above **Cala de Sant Esteve**; all this improvement results in a delightful 'pocket' sized walk taking in the infamous **Torre d'en Penjat** execution tower and the beautiful **Cala de Sant Esteve**. Unfortunately the buses still only run as far as **Es Castell** so bus users face an extra 3.5 kilometres, 1 hour, of pavement and lane walking, included in the PNF track.

3   1 H   3 km   100m / 100m   *   1

*Panhandle circular

Access by bus: To **Es Castell** terminus on the main ME-2 road and then walk south-east along the road.

Access by car: ME-2 through **Es Castell** and straight over the **Sol de Este** crossroads. Then take the narrow lane left and turn into the **Fort de Marlborough** car park.

Bus users head along the ME-2 pavement to the **Sol del Este** crossroads. Straight over the crossroads, we head towards **Bateria San Felipe** to take the narrow tarmac lane on the right heading for **Cala de Sant Esteve**. When the lane starts to run downhill we come to the car park entrance (left) and the cobbled Roman trail (right) to join our main route.

From the car park's elevated position we have an excellent view over the beautiful inlet of **Cala de Sant Esteve** and **Fort de Marlborough** (actually a redoubt rather than a fort, if we're feeling pedantic) to the brooding presence of **Torre d'en Penjat**; all of our walking route is laid out ahead of us - a unique tableau.

From the car park (Wp.1 0M) we step over the narrow lane to come onto the Roman trail (Wp.2) signed to 'Fort de Marlborough'. We drop down the steep boulder-laid trail to emerge onto the lane again at the head of the *cala* (Wp.3). Strolling along the lane beside the inlet, we swing left by house N°50 (Wp.4, and our return route) to walk up past **Fort de Marlborough** (Wp.5 8M) and curve round above a mini football pitch (12M).

Now our navigational skills are called into use as we leave the tarmac (Wp.6) to go left down concrete steps onto the limestone slabs and start curving round the headland on a stepped ascent through the old quarrying area, the **Torre d'en Penjat** coming into view ahead as we come up onto the sloping plateau (Wp.7 14M).

We follow a brown ribbon of a path running inland of the cliffs, keeping left at a path junction to pass on the seaward side of old stone walls dividing the plateau; farming has long ceased in this area, resulting in a natural habitat for flora and fauna, particularly butterflies. Fissures in the cliffs are eroding the headland so later walkers may need to move further inland as we come up to a path junction (Wp.8) where we go front right towards the tower. Coming through the remains of a building we climb steadily to a junction (Wp.9 22M) in front of a gated cave below the tower. Going left we climb up to the weathered metal steps of the **Torre d'en Penjat** (Wp.10 24M), where, from its weathered non-maintained appearance it gives the feeling that the local residents are choosing to ignore the tower in the hope that its notorious history will also disappear.

Leaving the tower we drop down to the junction (Wp.9) beside the gated cave, this time continuing straight ahead across the disused meadows and tumbled sections of stone walls to arrive at a T-junction of faint paths (Wp.11); amongst these walled meadows and *pistacia* bushes it is all too easy to wander aimlessly off track. Going left, right leads to a dead end, we curve right to squeeze through a cistus hedge (Wp.12) followed by a second squeeze hedge and a broken down wall as we keep to the worn path to emerge onto the **Camí de Sala** (Wp.13).

... a panoramic view ...

Navigation is now simplicity itself as we head down the rock and cobbled trail (N) to a panoramic view of the **Cala de Sant Esteve** before our trail drops steeply down and left below cliffs before dropping us onto the tarmac lane alongside house N°50 (Wp.4).

Now we have a short stroll to start of the **Roman Trail** (Wp.3) for its stiff climb, or a rather gentler ascent along the tarmac lane, back to the car park.

Looking for a short walk through wild countryside that takes in an easily accessible slice of Menorcan history? Then our Binissaida Circular is for you. Starting from the fortified **Binissaida** settlement, we pass through modern 'plotlands' before reaching the Hanging Tower of **Torre d'en Penjat**.

From the tower, we head south alongside the wild coastline until we turn inland to ascend through long abandoned farmland back to our starting point. (Note that although this final section of our route, Wps.12-18, is on abandoned farmland, it is private abandoned farmland. The landowner has not barred any access points but please respect his property.)

For a longer route, combine with our **Torre d'en Penjat** route (Walk 3, Guards, Guards!) to take in **Cala de Sant Esteve** and **Fort Marlborough**.

Access by car: On the ME-6 **Sant Lluís-Es Castell** road, turn off onto the **Binissaida** lane by the **Toraixer** farms. Drive carefully along the lane to the fortified **Binissaida de Damunt** farm to park alongside the lane. Please do not block any entrances off the lane. In the unlikely event of there being no off-lane parking at **Binissaida**, then turn round and follow our walking route our along the **Camí de sa Torra** dirt track towards **Villa Eugenia** and park where convenient.

From **Binissaida** (Wp.1 0M) we walk back down the lane passing the fortified **Binissaida de Damunt** behind trees on our right for a gentle stroll through a 'plotlands' development of walled and fenced market gardens. At the second crossroads of dirt tracks (Wp.2 6M) we turn right (E) onto the **Camí de sa Torra** where a ceramic wall plaque on the wall shows the layout of the plots

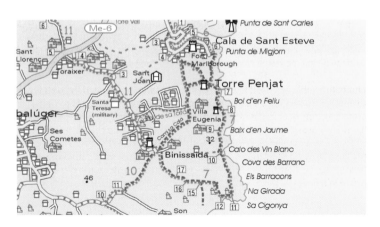

and tracks of the plotlands. Another easy stroll along the well stabilised track gives interesting views over the plots until we come up to the impressive entrance gates of **Villa Eugenia** (Wp.3 13M) to meet the cobbled trail of **Camí de sa Cala**. We could have walked down the **Camí de sa Cala** from **Binissaida** but it is becoming overgrown and even once you find its start, it offers negligible views. Alternatively, for a very short walk you can go right to follow it back to **Binissaida** (25M).

Torre d'en Penjat

Going left on the boulder cobbled *camí* we head down between stone walls until we come to a breach in the right hand wall (Wp.4 17M) where we take a clear path heading across abandoned farmland (E) toward **Torre d'en Penjat**. The brown ribbon path threads its way across the meadows and through gaps in stone walls until we come to a crossroads of paths (Wp.5) where we join our **Torre d'en Penjat** route as it leaves the tower. Going right, we follow the main path to come past a rock 'garage' from where we climb rock steps and a sloping path to the tower's metal entrance steps (Wp.6 24M).

(Unfortunately the steps have suffered some damage and corrosion, so take care if choosing to explore the tower's interior.)

Leaving the tower, (0M) we take a minor path running down towards the sea and cliffs beside a wall, and just before its end we turn through a stepped gap in the wall (Wp..7, built 1995). Above us is the impressive **Villa Eugenia** as we head (S) across open ground and limestone sheets to the makings of a path between a stone wall and the sea.

Heading south away from the tower

Our path establishes itself to push between feathery bushes and the wall for us to emerge from tamarisk and *pistacia* bushes by a mini-tower (Wp.8 11M); a civil war gun position with its crumbling barracks house. We pass below another villa as our path comes above the **Baix d'en Jaume**. Ahead, our path appears to end at intense vegetation, but as we get closer we find that a clear path winds its way through what appeared to be an impenetratable green barrier; so we don't need to go through the inland gate marked with green paint (Wp.9 17M).

Past the bushes, the path splits for a short section before rejoining to bring us around the head of a narrow inlet, **Caló des Vin Blanc**, to squeeze round the end of a stone wall above small cliffs (Wp.10 23M). Our path now climbs for us to pass through a wall as our route runs gently down paralleling the wall; our path dividing the foreshore from the old farmland inland as distant **S'Algar** comes into view. Our southern progress finishes at the wall's corner (Wp.11 32M) as our path swings right (W) to follow the wall to an old abandoned boathouse.

A beautiful line of limestone cliffs march south as our path starts to climb on a stony base, passing a path to an old well in a field on our right before we pass through an entrance (Wp.12 37M) into a bush-filled field. Our path contours across the long abandoned terraces to pass an abandoned cave dwelling before coming up to a Y-junction (Wp.13 39M), where we go left to climb steadily up to a gatepost topped with a cairn (Wp.14). Once this area was intensively farmed, but that was decades ago; these days the selling of 'plotlands' seems to be the economic activity of choice for most landowners.

Our trail heads up alongside a stone wall, passing a red-arrowed trail (Wp.15 44M) heading intriguingly (S) through an entrance, and keeping to the main trail to come through a wall entrance (Wp.16). If our earlier route is defined as 'plotlands' then this is certainly 'bushlands' as we come up past a superbly gnarled tree (Wp.17), our trail moving away from the stone wall (NW & then NNW). The tall bushes cut out the views apart from occasional glimpses of **Villa Eugenia's** 'palm avenue', so we keep to the main walked trail as it weaves between the bushes to come through a field entrance onto the access track to one of the **Binissaida** mansions (Wp.18 56M), **Es Barrancons**.

Turning left, we walk out through the gates onto the **Camí de Cavalls** main lane, which we follow round to the left and to a junction, where **Camí de sa Cala** starts away on our right (Wp.19), and then another couple of minutes sees us back at our start point.

Menorca's southern resorts, from **Binibèquer Vell** to **Punta Prima**, were once linked by a coastal trail. Development has turned much of this route into tarmac road with good pavements, which does make for easy strolling and requires few directions. For the final stage from **Biniancolla** to **Punta Prima** we take a coastal path, although even here there is an easier though much less interesting tarmac lane alternative.

While this is much more of a stroll than a hike our route contains many interesting features, most notable of which are the 'limestone tables' followed by the beautiful view down onto **Punta Prima** beach.

Access by bus: TMSA Route **Maó - Binibèquer**, return to **Maó** on the **Punta Prima** - **Maó** route (see appendices).

Access by car: On street parking in **Binibèquer**.

Short Version

Park in **Pas des Pescadores** (Wp.16) at **Biniancolla** and follow main route to **Punta Prima** beach and return.

We leave **Binibèquer Vell**'s commercial centre, set in the quaint reproduction 'Menorcan Fishing Village' development, (Wp.1 0M) and follow the coastal road's wide pavement eastwards until we turn right beside a roundabout onto **Calle de sa Platja** (Wp.2 12M) to overlook the rugged limestone foreshore followed by the white sands and azure seas of **Cala Binibèquer**; described by some holiday reps as "a beach in a Caribbean setting" - where do they get them from? Trails lead down to the beach, as we follow the road down into the valley behind the beach and up to a parking area with welcome seats for strollers (Wp.3 18M).

Continuing on the pavement, we turn right onto **Calle de sa Platja** (Wp4 22M) to stroll along overlooking the sea until we go onto a stepped path (Wp.5 25M) which brings us down to the dock of **Cala Torret**. Passing in front of the boat garages we take a tarmac lane to climb above the limestone shore and a pair of islands. As the narrow street drops down into the main bay of **Cala Torret**, we turn left on **Passeig des Porxos** (Wp.6), a tiled promenade lined with boat garages. We follow the *passeig* along the bay until the red tiling swings left by house Nº55 (Wp.7), where we continue straight ahead on a dirt track which serves the villas on the far side of the inlet. Past a traditional boat garage and below **La Familia**, the path runs along in front of the villas for us to return to the coastal road (Wp.8) by any of the access paths on our left.

From **Cala Torret** we have a relaxed stroll on pavements, following the traffic sign for 'Punta Prima, Biniacolla' (Wp.9) and passing an inlet opposite a road junction (Wp.10) followed by a beach house (Wp.11) and **El Caragol** (Wp.12 45M, and the halfway point for refreshments) before coming to the edge of

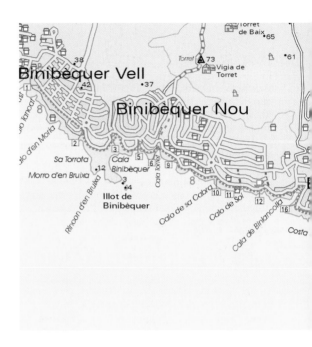

Biniancolla. Here we leave the 'main' road on a little seaward street (Wp.13) until opposite house N°39 (Wp.14) we go down over the open ground to the inlet before coming on to quarry tiled pavements. Going right at a T-junction (Wp.15 54M) to follow the **Passeig de sa Marina** around the inlet until it swings left (Wp.16), and an open cul-de-sac, **Pas des Pescadores**, is ahead of us.

Note:
If you want to take the easier route to **Punta Prima** at this point, then follow the street which runs behind the coastal villas.

Going down the cul-de-sac we turn left in front of a small villa built on a grass mound. At the **Villa Nevara** we follow the faint walking trail which runs along between the villas and the limestone shoreline. It's gently uphill on the faint and uneven trail, until we come to the unusual villa of circles with a shower at its apex. The trail now goes down in front of **Restaurant Son Ganzo** (Wp.17) to a set of villas in the twilight of their useful lives, a sharp inlet cutting into the coastline on our right. A pavement runs in front of the villas before we revert to the dirt trail which brings us up around newer villas to continue on the original trail - note that there are no villas on the seaward side of this route - to climb up onto the headland.

The coastal path skirts the villas as it runs along above the sharply jagged coastline, until we come to a major inlet. Here, the trail climbs up to a tarmac street (Wp.18 76M) to cross the inlet, and after the stone wall above the inlet, or at the first street light on the right, we go back down to the coastal trail. Our trail passes more jagged inlets before coming to the front door of a small villa faced with natural stone, where we begin the most geologically interesting

part of our route.

We step out onto horizontal limestone tables (Wp.19) which form a flat walking route.

On our left, the limestone has been weathered into a variety of shapes which show the thin, layered construction of the rock. Across the tabletop, the level on which we are walking now continues as a series of small, flat steps - be careful with your footing, and remember our advice, 'Look where you walk, and STOP to look at the view!'

The limestone tables

We come round to wider limestone tabletops and a pair of large boulders to overlook the beach at **Punta Prima** (Wp.20). The final stage is an easy stroll down the street, and not quite as easy across the sand (you could loop round on the road) to the beach front bars (Wp.21 91M) for some refreshment.

The south-east corner of Menorca from **Punta Prima** to **Alcalfar** and on to **S'Algar**, comprises one of the unspoilt coastal walks on the island. Combining good scenery, some impressive coastline, outstanding natural rock gardens, an immaculately restored fortified tower and a scenic refreshment stop, (in **Alcalfar**) this route is a must for everyone with well cushioned footwear. Expect to meet plenty of fellow walkers on Menorca's most popular coastal walking route.

Access by bus: TMSA bus from **Maó** to **Punta Prima**, return from either **Alcalfar** or **S'Algar** on the **Maó - Las Palmeras** bus (see appendices)

Access by car: On street parking in **Punta Prima**

Short Walk

To the **Xuroy** hotel terrace at **Alcalfar** and return, (80 minutes).

Starting out from where the **Punta Prima** development stops abruptly at the end of the beach (Wp.1 0M) we leave tourism behind us to stroll along the manicured trail which parallels the limestone-slab shoreline and a sandy track. When the concrete walkway turns inland to the new hotel we continue on a sandy path, passing an access to the sandy track before coming to a wall (Wp.2 5M) to swing right onto the *camí* track.

Our route runs alongside a substantial stone wall, inland of which is a wild, natural landscape, while all along our route you will find excellent specimens of endemic plants which thrive in this natural rock garden. We pass through a stone wall (Wp.3 10M) and our route narrows down to a walking trail which threads its way between the *pistacia* bushes. Faint paths lead off the main trail down towards the sea as our route becomes rougher.

As our trail climbs gently, the limestone-table shoreline is replaced by small cliffs, and we come to water run-off conduits built into the stone wall alongside our route. We follow the limestone track as it moves away from the sea and starts climbing to cross the headland. Limestone boulders are scattered like giant discarded weetabix on top of the table seashore, as we continue gently climbing up the trail.

Heading towards Torre d'Alcalfar Vell

An immaculate fortified tower comes into view (Wp.4), and the shoreline becomes more dramatic while we continue climbing up the headland. Before we reach the crest of the headland, a trail heads towards the tower. Here, we divert onto the minor trail and go towards the tower of **Torre d'Alcalfar Vell**.

Torre d'Alcalfar Vell has been so immaculately sanitised that it looks like Hollywood's idea of a tower, very different from the brooding presence of the 'execution tower' seen on our Walks 6 & 7. Walking around the base of the tower gives us excellent views across the south-east coastline. Leaving the tower, we take a walking trail which heads down towards the small inlet of **Caló Roig**. Our path, assisted by limestone steps, drops quickly down to come above the inlet with its undercut cliffs, the swell of the ocean causing the eroded cliffs to pant like an old dog. We come down alongside **Caló Roig**'s tiny beach to rejoin the main trail by an ancient well (Wp.5).

We leave **Caló Roig** behind as the trail climbs steadily onto the next headland in a series of limestone 'stairs'. Reaching the crest (Wp.6 27M), we look down on the beautiful inlet of **Cala d'Alcalfar** and its unusual limestone island with a natural tunnel through its centre. As we start descending from the crest we can clearly see the cliff structures of thin limestone slabs which combine to produce unusual layered geological sections. At a junction we continue ahead to walk above the inlet while across from us, large villas stand above traditional houses. We come through *pistacia* and cistus bushes to pass through a wall onto another trail (Wp.7 35M) where turning right brings us over a bridge and out into the car park at the rear of the **Hotel Xuroy**..

There are a number of alternatives to our official route off the headland. Going right at the path junction leads to a steep, stepped descent to the beach, while going left at Wp.7 junction leads back to Wp.5; both are alternatives if returning to **Punta Prima**.

Our main route continues up from the car park, though you might prefer to go down towards the beach and then come onto the terrace of the **Xuroy**, our favourite refreshment stop in this region. It would be a crime not to spend a little time here, enjoying a drink at this most scenic of inlets.
After our break at the **Xuroy** we have options of how we link with the path to **S'Algar**, or we can cut through to our Walk 10, 'From The New To The Old'.

Today, we take the steep concrete lane which goes up past an oil recycling collection point to come onto the village street of **Carrer de Levant**. Walking along the street and passing restored houses, we start climbing as we pass Nº18. A steady ascent brings us up to the level of the new villas as we go over the crest and stroll down to where the street turns sharp left. At this corner we go down onto the limestone slabs which form the top of the cliffs (Wp.8). Walking out across the slabs, we look back to see that the headland stands above a large cave.

There are no marked paths across the limestone as we walk above more large sea caves to pass on the seaward side of a white house. Past the house, we walk around more 'discarded weetabix' limestone slabs, to go left and join the main walking trail. We pass more 'weetabix' as we stroll across still more unusual rock slabs to come onto the rather sanitised seafront of **S'Algar** (Wp.9) either by going over a 'stone stepped' wall or opting for the easy gap in the wall. Drinks and food are available around the seafront swimming pool, and our Walk 10, 'From The New To The Old' starts here.

If you are walking to **S'Algar** and back on a warm day, you'll find the 'mass tourism' hostelries of **Punta Prima** a welcome sight at the end of your return route!

9A Short Cut to Walk 10

If you are linking the coastal route of Walk 9 with the inland route of Walk 10, then it's not necessary to sample the delights of **S'Algar** along the way. Here is a short cut route from **Alcalfar** which links the two walks.

(30 minutes, 1½ kilometres)

Walking up from the **Xuroy's** car park, we come onto **Alcalfar's** main street and continue along it until we come to a public telephone, where we turn left to walk up **Carrer Tramuntana** (sign on the first house on the left). It's a steady climb on the tiled pavement past small and large villas. Just before reaching the main road we go left on a little street, **Carrer de S'Ermita**, to walk along to a 'spaghetti western' church where we go up to cross the main road and walk away from **Alcalfar**. When we come to the impressive maroon presence of **Can Pancracio** we continue to the end of its garden wall, to turn right onto a dirt lane. As we walk down the lane past **Can Pancracio's** tennis court and vegetable plots, we can see the route of Walk 10, 'From The New To The Old', across the valley from us. The lane twists down into the small valley, and a gentle climb brings us up to cross the main road into **S'Algar** and onto the route of Walk 10.

10 FROM THE NEW TO THE OLD: S'ALGAR - BINISSAIDA (+ CALA D'ES RAFALET)

A largely restored **Camí de Cavalls** provides us with a delightful cross country route from **S'Algar** to **Cala de Sant Esteve.** This is an ideal route for dawdling, but do stay alert as we start closing with **Cala de Sant Esteve** as there are a number of direction choices to take; GPS waypoints are very useful here. Bus access is recommended for this long linear route.

If you are one of those who remembers our very first Menorca Walking Guide (1996), then unfortunately the public right of way at the start of this route has been closed off by the riding school at the **S'Algar Country Club**, and our old short route 10A is now walled off.

Access by bus: TMSA bus from **Maó** (see appendices)

Access by car: On street car parking at **S'Algar**. Drivers covering this linear route by car should park at **Es Castell** football ground (Wp.22), then bus to **Maó** bus station, change onto the **S'Algar** bus and then walk back to your car.

Short Walk

To **Cala des Rafalet** and return (2 walker, 25 minutes each way).

We start out from **S'Algar** seafront by walking up the road behind the seafront pool bar, to join the **San Lluís** road at a roundabout (Wp.1 0M). Continuing on the **San Lluís** road, we walk up to where a dirt track goes up through pine trees on our right (Wp.2 3M). Walk 9A, 'Short Cut To Walk 10' joins us from the dirt lane on the opposite side of the main road. We walk up the track (N) under the pines to pass **C'an Domir** on our left and continue gently uphill between a scattering of new and traditional houses to come up to a junction of trails (Wp.3 8M). On our right is our original 1996 route which now runs down to the country club and a second trail through the trees, while to our left the narrow entrance is now walled up (formerly Walk 10A in the 96 guide).

Our track levels out at the junction and then runs gently downhill, a lane going off to our right before we reach the end of vehicle navigation at a locked chain over a cattle grid (Wp.4). Taking care not to fall between the widely spaced bars, we cross the grid and step over the chain, to come into a woodland area. Following the track past a 'fire warning' sign we walk alongside a high stone wall, our track leads us down into a valley, stone walls now marking the right of our trail as it curves around an old limestone cutting area. Two gaps in the stone wall on our right lead to 'unofficial' paths across the sloping meadow down towards **Cala des Rafalet**.

Our track, now a limestone road, twists down past an old quarry to swing right onto a substantial stone bridge which spans the valley. At the far side of the bridge we come to the best known of the trails down to **Cala des Rafalet**, and the signboard for **Barranco de Rafalet** (Wp.5 15M).

Cala des Rafalet

It would be such a waste to miss the short excursion to **Cala des Rafalet** so we take the walking trail which drops steeply down beneath tree cover before taking on a gentler downhill nature along the steep valley. GPS reception is poor and runs out at Wp.6 as we come onto a stone shelf above the tiny beach.

We can edge around the rocks to get a better perspective of this beautiful inlet, before returning on the trail to rejoin our main route by the bridge. Ten minutes has been included in the main walk times for this diversion.

The limestone track gets rougher as we climb up from the bridge to a small electricity pylon (Wp.7 30M) to go onto a walking trail on our left. Passing beneath the pylon we come up to cross a stone wall, our trail running parallel to a stone wall across the open countryside before we step through a pedestrian entrance to come back onto the limestone track (Wp.8) in front of a chained entrance. Turning left, we stroll along the little-used lane with a shallow valley of neatly walled but abandoned fields on our right to come along to the imposing façade of **Rafalet Nou,** possibly the only traditional farmhouse on the island with a Greco-Roman extension!

At **Rafalet Nou** (Wp.9 33M) we go through rustic gates (not locked) to pass the house on our right as we continue on the limestone lane. It's an easy stroll along the lane between long-abandoned fields filled with thistles (or perhaps they farm the thistles?). Gradually we approach the entrance gates of **Rafalet Nou** to find them locked (this seems to be the normal situation). The easiest way past the gates is to use the *botadores* (wall steps) in the left hand wall and walk carefully along the wall to climb down outside the gates (Wp.10 40M). We come onto a tarmac lane where we turn right for an easy stroll along to the end of the lane at the entrance to **Son Vidal** (Wp.11 44M).

At the entrance to **Son Vidal** we take the old donkey trail, part of **Camí de Cavalls**, which is on our left. The donkey trail used to be choked with plants but has thankfully been cleared, though there are no views to either side or ahead until we come to the back of one of the traditional farmhouses, before we emerge from the **Camí de Cavalls** onto the end of a tarmac lane (Wp.12 52M). We follow the lane left, ignoring any dirt roads, to come around the farmhouse to its entrance where there is a *fuente*, and the lane swings right. The lane now goes past the classical 'fortified' farmhouse of **Binissaida**, although due to the high stone walls we can only enjoy a partial view of this classic structure from its entrance drive.

From the traditional farmhouses, we stroll down (N) between much newer weekender smallholdings, many with noisy guard dogs. Amongst this 'plotlands' style of rural development it is important not to miss our correct turnings if we are to reach **Cala de Sant Esteve**. **Camí d'es Ropit** (Wp.13) signed 'Hort de Lavi 7, 7A, 7B' is passed on our right at a crossroads before we come to **Camí de sa Torra** (Wp.14 61M) which we follow (E) to stroll along past more plotlands developments, keeping to the main *camí* track until we are facing **Villa Eugenia**, where we leave the main track to walk up to the impressive entrance gates and come onto the **Camí de sa Cala** (Wp.15 70M).

Turning left, we follow the walled donkey trail, pruners at the ready to cope with intrusive brambles, to a gap in the wall where a trail runs across towards the tower and then at a second gap (Wp.16) our trail from the **Torre d'en Penjat** joins us. Continuing down the donkey trail, we come out to overlook **Cala de Sant Esteve**; a stop to take in this beautiful scene is almost compulsory before we drop down steeply below cliffs to emerge onto the tarmac lane beside house N°50 (Wp.17 83M).

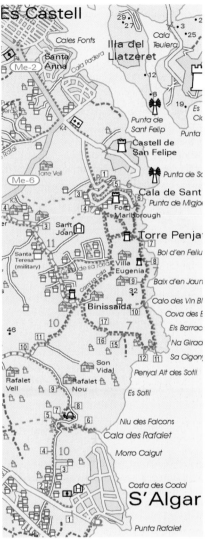

We stroll along the lane beside the *cala* to take the **Roman Trail** (Wp.18) beside a 'Fort de Marlborough' sign, to zigzag steeply up its cobbled surface. The gradient eases as we come back onto the tarmac lane (Wp.19 79M) beside the new **Fort de Marlborough** car park, though in wet weather, or if you wish a gentler ascent, we suggest that you stay on the tarmac lane. Now we crest a rise for an easy stroll along the narrow lane to meet the **Bateria San Felipe** road (Wp.20), where we go left to the **Sol de Este** crossroads (Wp.21). We are faced by a kilometre of pavement walking alongside the main ME-2 road, but not as bad as it sounds, to reach the **Es Castell** roundabout (Wp.22 99M) with 'Cales Fonts' signed right, and with the bus stop just past the junction.

This is possibly Menorca's easiest cross-country route, on a mixture of narrow tarmac lanes, dirt tracks and walking trails which, while brushing against modern developments retains a country air throughout its length. It is also one of the few routes that you could cycle as well as walk, though you will probably miss the final pedestrian short cut.

We intend this route as an alternative **Maó** finish for our **S'Algar - Camí de Cavalls** route (Walk 10) but you could walk it in reverse to access the **Binissaida** area from the island capital. Then again, the route is so relaxed, and relaxing, that you could enjoy it under the guise of 'stress relief'.

Access on foot: from walking routes which call at **Binissaida**.

We start at the collection of country farmhouses of **Binissaida** by the water trough (Wp.1 0M) to walk down the tarmac lane common to Walks 7 & 10, passing the fortified farmhouse on our right and then strolling through the plotlands until we reach the second crossroads of dirt tracks (Wp.2 6M). Here our other routes go right on the **Camí de sa Torra** while we keep straight ahead on the lane to pass the entrance to **Sant Joan** rural hotel on our right and the very silent **Santa Teresa** military listening post on our left. It is easy strolling along the lane past **Aubertonas** and **Can Fosc** before swinging right and left to reach **Can Jaxama** with its attractive ceramic seat (Wp.3 12M). After passing **Son Baix de Toraixer** and **Toraixer des Pi** country houses the tarmac lane swings right (Wp.4) while we continue ahead on a cobbled track lined with traditional farm houses to arrive at the ME-6 road (Wp.5 19M).

After scuttling carefully across the road we can relax on the **Camí de Biniatap** again as we pass **Sa Era de Toraixer** and a modern house on the right of the track before more bucolic strolling brings us to the **Camí de Rafal** (Wp.6 24M) off on our right; if you were to turn right here the track and lane will lead you onto the ME-6 shortly before the cemetery junction. Meanwhile we trundle along to the copse of tall trees marking **S'Hort des Pou** and an upmarket version of a 'plotlands' development.

Ceramic signs mark the route

Our rural tranquil finishes at a clutch of farmsteads followed by a road left to the *depuradora* (rubbish tip), a lane right to **Punt Verde** (recycling centre) and arriving at the corner of an industrial estate. Putting some extra pace in our step we come to cross the **Trepucó** road (Wp.7 37M).

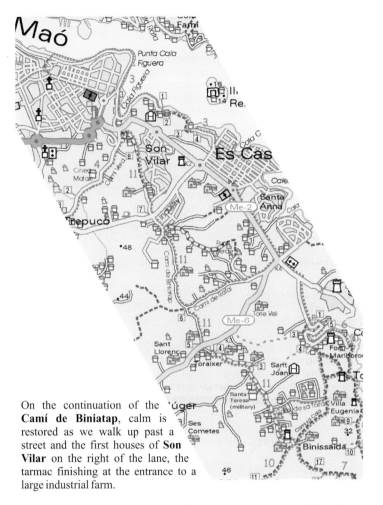

On the continuation of the 'úger Camí de Biniatap, calm is restored as we walk up past a street and the first houses of **Son Vilar** on the right of the lane, the tarmac finishing at the entrance to a large industrial farm.

The *camí* continues as a track/trail with the urbanisation hidden behind bushes until we drop down to the edge of **Son Vilar** again, the track becoming surfaced and a street goes right into the urbanisation opposite the **Camí de Biniatap** sign (Wp.8 46M). Now it's downhill, the patchy tarmac getting steeper as we pass houses on our left to come down behind ugly advertising hoardings. After the lane swings left behind the hoardings to run down the side of a valley to the **Camí Verd** road, we look for a gap in the mini-crash barriers (Wp.9) marking a steep staired pedestrian descent and path running out to the **Camí Verd** a few metres from its junction with the main road (Wp.10, 53M).

You have a choice of routes from the end of **Camí Verd**. Across the main road, the street down into **Cala Figuera** will take you onto our 'Town to Town' route (Walk 3), while going left up the main road will bring you to the edge of central **Maó** on the petrol station roundabout - well, we do have to return to urban reality eventually.

Don't be disappointed by the urban industrial landscape at the start of this walk; just wait for the dramatic change when we step out into the countryside on our 'Historical Tour'. For once hire-car drivers are well catered for, as the route can be made circular by using the outer road of the industrial estate, while bus users will appreciate the urban/rural contrast which comes from starting in **Maó**.

Access by bus: to **Maó** and follow Alternative Start.

Access by car: drive onto the industrial estate between the ME-1 and ME-12 roads west of **Maó**, and head for the western end of the estate to park near the **Pelaez** boat repair yard.

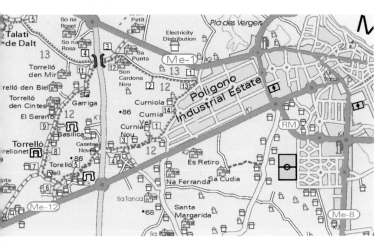

Alternative Start from Plaça de S'Esplanada in Maó

From **Plaça de S'Esplanada** we walk up **Carrer Vassallo** to go straight over the roundabout onto **Carrer Vassallo** to leave the old city behind, and come into the modern commercial suburbs. At the next roundabout (part of the RM ring road) we meet the industrial estate to walk along the quieter arterial road pavement. It is easy strolling along the estate's perimeter to reach its furthest point, two kilometres from **Plaça de S'Esplanada** and curve right to our start point opposite the **Pelaez boat** repair yard.

Leaving the estate's tarmac road (Wp.1 0M), we go down the **Camí Vell de Sant Clement** lane which swings left in front of the entrance lane to the **Refugi** dog pound. Ahead is a very different vista of bucolic rural charm, as we follow the lane up through a limestone cutting behind a smelly factory, to run out below an impressive outcrop Wp.2 4M). The lane continues below the outcrop towards the old farmhouse of **Curnia Vell**, while we go left onto a limestone donkey trail. It's gently uphill as the trail narrows to a walking path between old stone walls, bushes pushing in on our route. The bushes give way and the walls become lower to give us views across to the old farmhouse of **Curnia Nou** on our right, as our trail becomes a lane. Industry is not quite left behind, as we pass a large former quarrying area where some of the excavated caves have become industrial storage units as we come along to the entrance to **Curnia Nou**, where a tarmac lane comes in from our left (Wp.3 8M).

We continue straight ahead on a rough stone lane, still the **Camí Vell de Sant Clement**, passing an electricity substation on our right as we climb up to pass **Villa Francisco** - a traditional white farmhouse - and another fifty metres brings us up to a busy main road (Wp.4 11M). We cross with care, going straight over onto the continuation of **Camí Vell de Sant Clement** which runs into the small village of **Ses Casetes Noves** (not signed). Following the lane as we head between the impressive houses, the lane becomes less used after house Nº25, the tarmac then finishing at **Turo Can Rabul**.

Our route continues along an overgrown track to come to a traditional *camino real* donkey trail. This is one of our 'rescued by pruning' donkey trails where we spent some time with secateurs re-establishing the trail. Be prepared to push through some foliage, and please bend back or prune the bushes and brambles. Keeping this route open is important, as the alternative route involves walking along busy main roads without pavements.

The start of the *camino* is relatively clear as we walk down between high stone walls. Brambles become prominent (please prune) for fifty metres, before the trail goes right by a field entrance. We go gently downhill through a leisurely S-bend, passing an old farmstead on our left. Our trail runs down to mature trees on our right which clothe the remains of a hut, before running along to join a lane below a traditional white farmhouse (Wp.5). The stony lane climbs up to reach a crest with a house and a barn on our left, before running downhill towards the airport landing lights. A small rise brings the lane up to join a tarmac lane under the array of landing lights (Wp.6 22M).

We turn right and then take the narrow lane **Camí de Torello** signed to 'El Sereno restaurant'. Our track runs gently uphill between stone walls to go across the landing lights, and weaves its way through the countryside. At another sign for **El Sereno** we pass the **Camí de Mussulá** off on our left (Wp.7) as we come in sight of the **Torrelló** *talaiot*, unique for the window on its summit. From our viewpoint, the *talaiot* also appears to have a modern chimney! Another 100 metres brings us up to one of Menorca's largest *talaiots* and its unusual entrance (Wp.8 27M).

The **Torrelló** *talaiot* is contained within a high stone wall with a narrow flight of traditional wall steps (*botadores*) providing access onto the wall by the signboard. From the top of the wall there's an even more precipitous flight of steps into the compound. The descent and the climb back out, together with the traversing of the compound, call for a high level of agility, and if you have any doubts on this score, we would advise you not to go down the narrow steps. Also within the compound are some well shafts covered with discarded pallets, and many of the stones are less secure than they appear - perhaps a less friendly archaeological site than most!

From the *talaiot* we continue down the lane; note that the entrance to **Torellonet Vell**, passing between farmhouses and fields is private. As the lane levels out past the houses, we see an unusual modern structure away on our right, an easy stroll bringing us to the junction of **Fornas de Torrelló** (Wp.9) with its parking area and bike rack.

Mosaic detail at Fornas de Torrelló

Leaving the main lane, we stroll along to the basilica mosaic (Wp.10) that is housed below a modern roof. Once the floor of an early Christian church (6th century AD), the repeated bird patterns are well preserved.

Unfortunately, the chain-link fencing and opaque perspex which protect the area make the taking of good photographs from the elevated viewing walkway tricky.

After examining the mosaic we retrace our steps and rejoin the lane, turning right towards **El Sereno**. A gentle downhill stroll brings us down to the restaurant, only open from 20.00-23.00 hours and from May to October. Our trail continues gently uphill, passing new villas on our left as the lane becomes rougher underfoot, then running along between **Ses Llurenses** and **Sa Garriga** farmhouses. Leaving the farmhouses behind, we sneak off downhill past another palatial residence for us to come down to the junction of lanes (Wp.11 46M) on the route of Walk 13, 'More Historical Sights'.

Walk 13 goes left while we drop down to go under the main road. Emerging from the tunnel, the lane undulates along to another junction (Wp.12), where the main lane runs down to the ME-1 main road, while we take the track right, paralleling the ME-1, to pass **Son Cardona Nou** on our right. Our route undulates along through the countryside, the stone walls high on one section, passing the electricity distribution transformers on our left before curving round a large spinney.

The lane starts to descend gently towards the industrial estate, unfortunately accompanied by industrial dumps alongside the track, to emerge onto the perimeter road by a car storage depot (Wp.13 62M) and the TAS depot. Car drivers should follow the perimeter road right to a roundabout (Wp.14) where we go right to return to our start point and parked car (Wp.1 70M). Bus users will find it easiest to go over onto **Calle 6** and cut through the estate to rejoin our outward route for the return into **Maó**.

13 MORE HISTORICAL SIGHTS: MAÓ - TALATÍ DE DALT - RAFAL RUBÍ VELL

This walk follows a mixture of country lanes linking an important *talaiot* and *taula* site with the best preserved *navetas* on the island. Much of the walking is on narrow tarmac lanes, although the start is on a much rougher 'four wheel drive' track.

| 3 | 3 H | 12 km | 50m ↗ 50m ↘ | ⟷ and return | 0 |

Access by bus: to **Maó** bus station, then follow Walk 12 Alternative Start and the reverse route of Walk 12 to our start.

Access by car: as for Walk 12 but continue around the estate to park near the TAS depot.

Our starting point is opposite the TAS depot on the edge of the industrial estate (Wp.1 0M) where we take the track (E) to start out walking between the plots and builders yards. Once the yards finish (Wp.2) our track becomes rougher and runs through pleasant countryside to take us past the entrance to **Sa Punta de Sant Clement** and **Son Cardona Nou** farmhouse before coming out onto the **Camí Vell de Alaior** tarmac lane (Wp.3 12M). Turning left we walk up under the bridge carrying the main road to a T-junction (Wp.4 16M) where the **Camí de Torello** goes left, while we go right to continue on the **Camí Vell de Alaior**.

We start out along the rough country lane, **Camí Vell de Alaior**, which parallels the ME-1 **Maó-Alaior** road. Our route runs through wild abandoned countryside, climbing gently past field entrances on our left. Blackberries are taking over the stone walls, and the lane's surface becomes solid limestone, not always flat, before resuming its rough surface to run downhill between stone walls to a pair of field entrances. The views over the fields, mostly of thistle, improve as we walk along towards a radio transmitter mast. We climb gently on limestone slabs and laid boulders up to a crest between a large limestone outcrop and the radio mast, to come out on a tarmac lane (Wp.5 27M). Turning left we stroll along to the purple sign at the entrance to **Talatí de Dalt** (Wp.6 30M).

Talatí de Dalt

To reach the archaeological site, we cross a stepped wall and follow a grass and boulder track up to the site entrance. Going clockwise round the rock mound, we come to the unusual standing stone which makes this site unique. A sloping stone is set to support the 'T' piece - or could it be part of a stone ring which has slowly toppled over three millennia? It's an easy climb to the top of the stone mound from where we enjoy views over the countryside and away to the **Ermita Mare de Deu del Toro** on Menorca's only mountain. **Talatí de Dalt**, along with most other *talaiot* sites, gives the impression of having been only cursorily investigated, this view being supported by the large cave hidden by a tree near the site entrance.

From **Talatí de Dalt** we continue along the narrow tarmac lane (W) past **Al Sendro Vell** with views across to the restored farmhouse and buildings of **Algendaret** set on a limestone outcrop

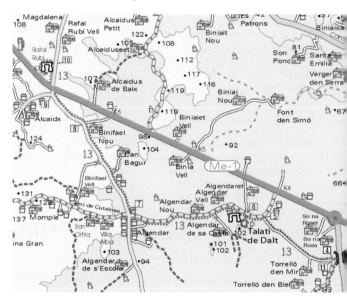

Our route wriggles around an outcrop of limestone to come past excellent specimens of wild flowers and to an electricity substation. The lane swings left and climbs gently up alongside **Algendar Vell**.

Over the crest of the rise, we pass a gated track on our left, followed by the restored farmhouse **Algendar Nou** on our right as we stroll gently downhill. Blackberry brambles and bushes restrict our views as the lane twists between stone walls and past a patch of wild dog roses to come to a woodland area. Ahead is a square tower, our lane gently rising for us to come up to the electricity substation and farms on a crossroads of the lanes (Wp.7 51M).

Ahead is **Camí de Coutaines** while we turn right to walk down the 'main' narrow lane which runs between low stone walls allowing views over this rural landscape. We pass **Sa Cometa de Algendar** farm on our left, followed by the entrance to **S'Espinal**; though unfortunately the Dragon Tree noted in our previous editions has now gone, to be replaced by a vase set in the wall. We have an easy stroll along the lane, passing more wild dog roses and the entrance to **Biniafael Vell** before cresting a rise and coming down between trees to cross a shallow valley. We then climb over another crest beside **Biniafael Nou** to come to a junction (Wp.8 67M) where the **Camí de**

Biniafael track goes right. Continuing on the main lane we come along to a T-junction (Wp.9 74M) by an electricity tower to swing right down to the ME-1 main road.

We carefully cross directly over the ME-1 onto the **Camí de Rafal Rubí** country lane; take particular care as traffic is fast on this section of road, and only cross when it is completely clear. On this final section the *navetas* of **Rafal Rubí Vell**, are clearly in sight on our left as we keep on the lane to pass the first *naveta*, following the land owner's signs along to a rustic gate entrance (Wp.10).

Through, or over, the gate, we come onto a small path which runs along the edge of a cornfield to the first of the *hypostyle* chambers, a well-preserved example that you can crawl into, its stone-slab roof supported on pillars; rather surprisingly sponsored by Spar supermarkets! The path continues into another field where we find the larger of the *navetas* (Wp.11), a boat-shaped burial chamber constructed from limestone boulders.

In common with the other archaeological sites, there are no refreshments to be had at **Rafal Rubí**, the nearest possibility being the CEPSA service station shops, another two hundred metres along the main road. Our return is back along our outward route, making for a long country walk through the beautiful, tranquil rural landscape.

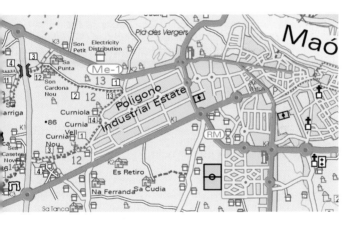

S'Albufera - a haven for wildlife

The **S'Albufera** wetlands reserve has three short waymarked walks designed to give views of this protected *Parc Natural* area. The red and green routes both start from the end of the tarmac in the failed urbanization of **Santa Modrono**. To reach the start, drive out of **Es Grau** and take the first turning right, signed to **S'Albufera** reserve.

Past the information office on your left, keep straight ahead on the tarmac until it runs out at a parking area marked by a signboard (Wp.RG1). The blue route begins from the **Es Grau** car park. All routes are graded 1 Walker strolls - and don't forget your binoculars.

Red Route (30 minutes)

From the signboard (Wp.RG1) we head east , climbing over a stone wall by means of its steps and walking up a rough dirt road to a marker post, and then on to cross another wall (Wp.R2) before coming to a junction (Wp.R3). A marker post directs us straight ahead (E) to a signboard illustrating some of the local endemic plants species found in this area (Wp.R4), and on to cross another stone wall with steps.

We come outside villa number 164 sitting in splendid isolation (Wp.R5), and then our route swings left to pass a chained entrance (Wp.R6) and run down to a saddle and then up to overlook the lagoon. On this final stage, we have *mirador* views over the reserve as our dirt road curves round to finish at a signboard, this time describing some of the birds to be seen in this area (Wp.R7 15M).

We retrace our route to return to the parking area.

Green Route (15 minutes)

From the car park and signboard (Wp.RG1), we cross a wall to head NW on a wide dirt road which curves left to a Y- junction which is dominated by a large green sign (Wp.G2). A marker post sends us along the right road and over a wall by using its steps to walk between large bushes (N), going gently uphill to a T-junction with an almost blank marker post. We go left (SW,) and our route narrows to a walking trail before it comes onto another dirt road. *Mirador* views open up as we come to a signboard providing information about some of the bird life of the area (Wp.G3). A marker post directs us up a walking trail, and climbing up through the undergrowth brings us to another marker post (Wp.G4 10M).

Here, a green arrow points ahead, but a line of stones across the path shows that we should take the clear path to our right. Pushing through thorny broom we come onto a broad dirt trail (Wp.G5) where a marker post shows three (confusing) directions.

Going left, we drop down past an abandoned villa to the Y-junction with the green signboard (Wp.G2). From here we have an easy stroll back along our outward route to the car park (15M).

Blue Route (25 minutes)

Starting from the **Es Grau** car park (Wp.B1 0M), we follow the route of Walks 15 and 16 across the **S'Albufera** stream to head across the beach until we turn left at its northern end onto the **S'Albufera** path (Wp.B2), to stroll up to a *mirador* sign (Wp.B3) on the sandy track. Easy strolling brings us to a plant information board (Wp.B4), a blue waymark pointing back along our route as we continue on past another sign board (Wp.B5) to come to the start of the **S'Albufera**'s impressive walkway over the water (Wp.B6)

From here, we have a choice of walking over the water or following the woodland path (PNF track follows the woodland path). The two routes come together again at the end of the walkway (Wp.B7), from where we stroll through the trees to cross a bridge (Wp.B8). All too soon we are leaving the **S'Albufera** (Wp.B9), to walk back down the road to the **Es Grau** parking area.

S'Albufera des Grau - the Nucleus of the Biosphere Reserve

The entire island of Menorca was declared a Biosphere Reserve by UNESCO in 1993, centred upon **S'Albufera des Grau**. It earned its status for its conservation of the environment and wildlife, and its protection of its historical and cultural heritage.

The **Natural Park of S'Albufera des Grau** covers an area of over 5000 hectares, of which 1750 are aquatic. In addition to its resident bird population, an amazing diversity of migratory species use the area as a stopover.

For more information, ask in the Tourist Offices for their information leaflet, 'S'Albufera des Grau'.

The **Es Grau** peninsula area has much to offer in addition to its beach, village and waterside bar/restaurants. Our first walk in this area takes us along an idyllic coastline dotted with pocket-sized beaches.

If nineteen GPS waypoints looks like a lot for an hour's walk, this is because the peninsula has a myriad of paths and it is all too easy to stray onto another route in this terrain.

$$**\text{Panhandle circular}$$
$$* \text{ in } \textbf{Es Grau}$$

Access by bus: very limited - only from July to September, from **Maó**. Check in Bus or Tourist Offices on current availability when you arrive on the island.

Access by car: From the ME-7 road turn off onto the ME-5 road signed to **Es Grau** and park in the car park at the start of the village.

Starting from the car park at the entrance to **Es Grau** (Wp.1 0M) we walk a few steps down the road to turn onto the beach. Crossing the stream from **S'Albufera** we head across the beach to come onto a broad dirt and rock path (Wp.2) which climbs up onto the headland. We pass a path (Wp.3) and cross over a saddle to come into the next valley, where we pass a second path (Wp.4) which drops to the valley floor. Passing another path off to our right (Wp.5), we come amongst trees (14M) to go through a stone wall (Wp.6) on a gradual ascent up the wooded slope.

At fifteen minutes (15M) a small path goes off to our left (Wp.7), while we stay on the main path which curves up through the trees (NNW). We come out of the trees to a trail junction (Wp.8) and then on to a gap in a stone wall (Wp.9 20M), our path narrowing as it reaches the high point of this section of the route.

Now we come gently down (E) past a path off to our right (Wp.10), and losing **Es Grau** before a gentle rise brings the village back into view, and our path heads towards the houses across the water. At a T-junction (Wp.11 24M) we go left (ENE), and left again at another fork (Wp.12) to head towards **Illa d'en Colom** (ENE). A stony path (Wp.13) takes us down towards a tiny beach, and we then stroll along above azure waters, passing below a cave house before passing through a wall (Wp.14).

After a short drop, our stony path angles away from the straights and past the last of the tiny beaches which face **Illa d'en Colom**, to bring us up onto the rocky headland (32M). The headland is a trackless area, so we take our direction towards an old tower (Wp.15) before curving (SW) towards a sandy beach to come onto a discernible path (Wp.16).

Coming alongside an inlet (S) we swing right across its head (Wp.17) and then cross over a saddle to go down the narrow path (Wp.18) with pampas-like grasses and *pistacia* bushes pushing in on our route before we reach the beach. It's a good idea to take a break on this quiet beach before tackling our return route.

Pistacia lentiscus

From the end of the beach, we head inland on a small rough path (Wp.19) which soon climbs intensely. It's a stiff climb up the valley to meet our outward route once more (Wp.7 50M) to retrace our outward route, the waterside bars of **Es Grau** proving a powerful magnet to guide us back to base (65M).

Illa d'en Colom

The **Illa d'en Colom**, along with the **Illa d'Addaia** (further north up the Menorcan coast), is home to the indigenous plant *Daphne rodriguez* and also the lizard species *Podarcis lilfordi* which is thought to be the only species of vertebra still inhabiting Menorca which pre-dates the arrival of the first human settlers, although it has now evolved into several unique varieties.

Menorca is rich in archaeological sites, but **Torre Blanca** is one of the most interesting, perhaps made more so because it has not been manicured. Add to this a varied route taking in coastline and country meadows for a great value walk.

Refreshments are available only at the start and end of this walk, so take food and drink with you.

Panhandle circular * in Es Grau

Access by bus: very limited - only from July to September, from **Maó**. Check in Bus or Tourist Offices on current availability when you arrive on the island.

Access by car: From the ME-7 road turn off onto the ME-5 road signed to **Es Grau** and park in the car park at the start of the village.

Starting from the car park at the entrance to **Es Grau** (Wp.1 0M) we walk a few steps down the road to turn onto the beach. Crossing the stream from **S'Albufera** we head across the beach to come onto a broad dirt and rock path (Wp.2) which climbs up onto the headland. Passing a path (Wp.3) we climb over a saddle to come into the next valley, where we pass a second path (Wp.4) which drops to the valley floor. Passing another path off to our right (Wp.5), we come amongst trees (14M) to pass through a stone wall (Wp.6) on a gradual ascent up the wooded slope.

At fifteen minutes we go left on a small path (Wp.7 15M) while the main path continues curving up through the trees. As we emerge from the foliage we look down on the idyllic bay of **Fondeadero de los Llanes**. A narrow, steep path drops us down the sharp valley before running out to join a coastal path at the end of the beach (Wp.8 20M).

Crossing the beach, we climb up (NW) to a gap in the wall (Wp.9) and then drop down the left hand path which brings us onto a track (Wp.10). Going right, we have an easy stroll along the track and past a wetlands lagoon with a tower ahead of us (NE), our route then swinging away from a beach (Wp.11 30M) to head north-west into a new valley.

As we top a rise (Wp.12) the sea comes back into view, and we stroll down past a beach before climbing up to pass an old cottage (Wp.13). We then drop down to the swampy region alongside **Cala de sa Torreta** (37M) and our track, now sandy, runs in amongst pine trees and swings right (Wp.14 SW) to emerge facing a boat house. Our track swings left to climb gently away from the sea for us to come up through a gate entrance (Wp.15 41M) as our track steadily ascends through meadows to a saddle (45M), before descending gently (NW).

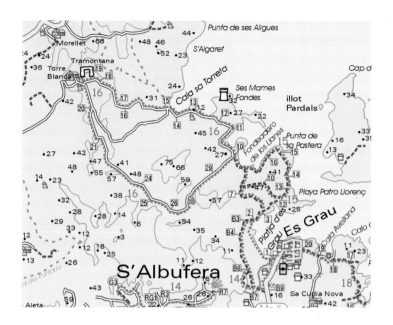

We pass a drinking trough, then go through another gate entrance (Wp.16 50M).

Torre Blanca *poblat*

Now it's a steady ascent through another entrance (Wp.17) and then alongside a stone wall, until we pass through yet another entrance (Wp.18 58M) where we catch a glimpse of a modern farm building which indicates that we are finally closing with the

The *Taula* at Torre Blanca

Torre Blanca *poblat*. We come up to the farm buildings, turning up to the gate by the breeze block barn. A path on the right of the gate leads around the building to the *poblat* of **Torre Blanca** (Wp19 60M).

The dappled shade provided by overhanging trees enhances the site's archaeological interest, making this one of Menorca's most attractive historic sites, and just the place to take a break before starting our return to **Es Grau**.

We begin our return (0M) by heading south from the farmyard through a gate with a cloth tie closure and onto a little-used dirt lane, which brings us to gates on our right latched with a wooden stake (Wp.20). Going through the gates, we come over a little rise, and then down through a field entrance to parallel an old donkey trail stuffed with *pistacia* bushes. After passing through another pair of gate posts (Wp.21 10M) we descend between stone walls before emerging to views across wooded valleys (Wp.22). Passing a track down to our right (Wp.23), we then drop down into the next valley with views over **S'Albufera**, to go through yet another set of gate posts (Wp.24).

Our path is now little-used and bordered by an abundance of wild flowers, as we pass a water trough and gate posts (Wp.25), almost at the waters of the **S'Albufera**. We cross a stream in the next field as our route swings ESE to pass through more gate posts (Wp.26) and ascend gently to a well alongside the track (Wp.27 30M). Once past the well, we face a steady ascent over a crest (Wp.28) before strolling downhill once more. Rope-latched gates (Wp.29) mark a distinct change from farmed to wild countryside, and we stroll down between slopes reclaimed by nature to meet our outward route (Wp.10).

Now we retrace our outward route back to the southern end of the beach (Wp.8) to take the inland path. It's a stiff climb up the valley to meet our **Es Grau Peninsula** route (Wp.6 50M) amongst the trees. Again, we retrace our outward route, looking forward to the pleasures of the hostelries at **Es Grau** after more than two hours of exploration.

Many visitors get to **Cap de Favaritx**, but they only explore the immediate area. Follow our walk and you'll be rewarded by deserted beaches, a wild untouched coastline, and a bird-watcher's paradise. Remember to take along a picnic, as you will be a long way from refreshments.

3   1½ H   4.5 km   170m 170m   and return   0

Access by car: From the ME-7 we drive north-east on the country lane serving **Cap de Favaritx**. When the lane swings east, start looking for the rustic gates on the right of the lane which mark the start of our route, and seek out a parking place alongside the lane. Potentially busy at weekends, but often quiet or deserted on weekdays.

We walk around the rustic gates (Wp.1 0M) to come onto a broad stony track which heads through the slate landscape, climbing gently and gradually curving (SW-W) amongst the stone, shrub-clothed dunes (Wp.2 10M).

We come to a junction (Wp.3 12M) where a rough track continues ahead we swing left on the main track (S) to come onto a rise overlooking **Cala Presili**, with Menorca's eastern coastline disappearing into the misty distance. Now it is gently down through zigzags (short cuts are possible) to the end of the road above the beach (Wp.4 15M).

Paths take us down to **Cala Presili** where polished slate and pebbles line this small beach at the mouth of the valley. From the southern end of the beach we can either take a path which climbs steadily up the northern side of a small valley, or the steeper ascent over open ground (on a faint path) onto the headland (Wp.5 23M) to look down on the beautiful and probably deserted beach of **Platja de Capifort**.

The Aveagua wetlands.

Inland from the beach are the **Aveagua** wetlands where bird watchers should seek a comfortable vantage point amongst the high dunes.

A variety of paths take us slip-sliding down through the high dunes (S), or we can take a cliff-side path down to an old wall (Wp.6) to come onto the impressive beach (30M). It is easiest to follow a route alongside the lagoon's vegetation to reach the end of the beach (Wp.7), where we take a small path which climbs up the headland. After fifty metres we have a choice of routes (Wp.8); either straight up, or continuing on the main path for a gentler ascent.

Once on the top, we continue south-east, to overlook a small bay as we head down to an old wall. After going through the wall (Wp.9 28M), we gently ascend (E/SE) to the top of the cliffs (Wp.10 43M) and stroll along to a small plateau on **Cap de Ses Piques**, overlooking **Cala Morella Nou** (45M), a beautiful and isolated spot from which to enjoy the tranquil side of Menorca.

To return, we retrace our outward route.

On a map, this route looks like an easy stroll up the east coast of Menorca - not a bit of it! Government maps show the **Camí de Cavalls** in this region - not a sign of it! It looks flat on the map but the reality is lots of ups and downs, combined with numerous decision points where it is all too easy to go wrong! Trails are generally rough and the low, scratchy bushes intrusive, even tempting us fashionistas into thinking the unthinkable and considering gaiters! When we do get to **Es Grau** the easiest option for getting back to **Cala Mesquida** is to walk back down the route, but at least by then you will have ironed out any wayfinding problems and be better able to enjoy the dramatic scenery.

In short, this is a route for experienced walkers, prepared to follow our detailed walk description to the letter, who are up for a challenge. **Es Grau** has a clutch of welcoming bars, and if you really want to make a long day of it, add Walk 15 or 16 to your itinerary before returning. GPS Waypoint navigation is a great help, particularly for walking the route in reverse.

Note: Much, or possibly all of this route is over military or private land but all accesses were open at October 2004. Do not stray inland from our 'official' route.

Access by car: From **Maó** take the ME-3 road and turn off to **Cala Mesquida**. Continue through the village (slowly) and out to the end of the road at **Platja Mesquida** to park on the beach.

We start out from the end of the road (Wp.1 0M) by walking along the beach (NE) to the start of a path between boulders. The path soon runs out as we make our way across open ground to a pedestrian gap in a substantial stone wall (Wp.2 4M) to walk across the top of the pebble beach and open ground (W) and come onto a track (Wp.3 7M) at the edge of the military area. Turning right, we drop down to come behind the end of the beach, the track already deteriorating to a trail, to climb steeply (N) up to the first crest (Wp.4 16M); a taster of what the route involves. We are back to track width as we drop down into a bush-filled valley before climbing gently onto the next headland (Wp.5 21M).

We are looking down into a tranquil valley, pebble beach, boathouse and islets looking like basking whales; these distractions making it all too easy to swing inland on the track. Don't! It leads eventually, via ascents/descents and increasing smells, to the high fence of the *depuradora* and possible interviews with the military; we know.

Look for an arrow of stones pointing (N) along a faint path. Down the path we come to a faint junction and choice of routes. Safest is to go front left and down, to clamber over a stone wall and continue to the valley floor by an old well. More adventurous, but certainly not so safe, is to continue ahead to come to the end of the wall by a giant fracture in the cliff face (Wp.6). We can clamber over the wall, or gingerly step onto the huge fracture and quickly off again on the opposite side of the wall. (Note: If this fracture has fallen into the sea, backtrack to the safe route.) We then have an open ground descent to join the safe route and then walk across the pebbles to the boat house (Wp.7 27M).

Just inland of the boathouse we go through a gate with a height bar to start climbing straight up the slope (N) on a faint trail. At the top of the cliffs we have excellent views as a reward for our effort before continuing on (NNW) climbing gently, the faint path splitting and rejoining before we come to the end of the second bush-covered height on our left (Wp.8 42M). Now our faint trail swings inland (W) over a faint junction to come up to a broken down section of stone wall (Wp.9 46M). Turning right (N) we climb up across a small field to an entrance in the wall to find ourselves outside the remains of a stone hut (Wp.10, 48M).

... ahead is a second boathouse ...

Leaving the ruin behind, we come down to skirt a bush-covered hump on its seaward side, our path coming above the cliffs (risk of vertigo) to a rock cube (Wp.11 54M) making for an excellent *mirador* rest point if you have a head for heights. Ahead is a second boat house, as we navigate down over open ground to come down into a gentle valley.

Before reaching the boathouse, do not make the mistake of peering into the 'well', as you'll soon find that it's a privy!

While the existence of a boathouse (Wp.12 63M) might give the impression of some degree of civilisation, there are no onward paths evident. A stone wall climbs up the side of the valley running inland. Feel like a hillock? Well so did we as we pushed up from the wall through bushes and scrambled over a wall, only to find a well stabilised dirt track which we would have come onto if we had stayed following the wall! Up the track, we come to a T-junction (Wp.13 75M) with the dirt road remains of the abandoned **Sa Cudia Vella** urbanisation.

Turning right, we follow the remains of the dirt road round to *mirador* views along the coastline. This is easy strolling, and it looks as if our wayfinding problems are behind us as we pass a pair of tracks off to our left and our route starts curving towards the east to overlook neat fields and a nest box mounted on a large pole beside a neat stone wall. Best not to relax too much, as we need to find our onward path (Wp.14 96M) as the track continues curving uphill.

Our path runs down to cross a tumbledown wall (into the seaward edge of the **Sa Cudia Nova** estate) and then starts climbing gently (NE-N), our route confirmed by a cairn as we push through the bushes on the stone littered path. When the path disappears on solid rock, we keep heading north to start descending towards a 'limestone bar', another cairn confirming direction before crossing a grassy area to step onto the 'bar' (Wp.15 113M). The wayfinding is little easier ahead so we take a break to admire the impressive coastline.

From the end of the 'bar', cairns mark our ascent (NW) up to cut through a wall (Wp.16 117M) to the edge of a small steep valley. Now we pick our way down into the valley to cross a path running along the valley floor, followed by a steep climb up the northern wall. Occasional cairns confirm our route as approximately north through the scrub to crest a rise overlooking the **Es Grau** inlet, a picky descent bringing us down to join a better defined trail (Wp.17 134M); make a note of this point if you will be returning to **Cala Mesquida** on foot.

Turning left (W) on the better trail we head along towards the roofs and antennae of **Es Grau** to come onto a track (Wp.18 137M) which runs between a well and a boathouse before starting a steady ascent. While climbing up the track, it's easy to miss the path off the track (Wp.19) which takes us down across a small beach before climbing up through bushes, keeping left at two junctions, then coming to stones set beside a stone wall to assist our crossing onto a street (Wp.20 146M). Civilisation at last, as we go right and then left to walk down **Carrer de Llevant** to its end (Wp.21 149M) opposite houses N°s 13, 15 & 17, where the nearest bar is a few metres to our right.

Menorca's west coast is very poorly served with walking routes, so it is a double pleasure for us to find an open access trail linking **Cala Blanca** to **Cap d'Artrutx**, and that the route has not been previously published in any guide book that we've seen. Our route is straightforward, rather than exciting, with some 'almost open ground' navigation, but forms an important link along the coast where none previously existed.

While we walk the route from **Cala Blanca** 'down'(meaning south down the map rather than downhill) to **Cap d'Artrutx**, we envisage that it will be used mainly as a relaxed day out from the resort area on the south-east corner, by walking up to the beautiful small bay and beach of **Cala Blanca**, flanked by laid-back bars and restaurants, and returning after lunch by the same route.

* 4 when done in reverse

Access by bus: Catch the **Ciutadella** bus From **Cap d'Artrutx** roundabout and ask for **Cala Blanca**. From the **Cala Blanca** stop, walk down the ME-24 and go left down to the junction above the bay, go left over the bridge and follow the street above the bay until it turns sharp left; here is the start of our trail. Add 1¼ kilometres and 15 minutes walking time, shown as the green' Alt' route on map. For bus times, see the appendices at the back of this book.

Access by car: Turn off the ME-24 at the **Cala Blanca** junction and follow the 'Access by Bus' notes. There is plenty of on-street parking along the street leading to the start of our trail.

At the end of **Avinguda Ponent** (Wp.1 0M) as the street swings left, we step off the pavement promenade onto a clear trail that runs out across the rock and bush desert. Our route follows the rocky coastline to pass through a gap in a stone wall (Wp.2 5M), a dirt track running inland before we pass through a second wall to come onto limestone slabs forming a plateau above the low cliffs. Following the mud-streak trail (S) across the open ground, the route splits, both parts heading south-west, before rejoining to continue past rock wind shelters for sun worshipers. The route's surface becomes a mixture of rock and earth as we pass a faint trail off to the largest stone wind shelter, just before coming to a gravity gate set in a stone wall (Wp.3 13M).

The well at Wp.4

Once through the gate - or over the broken down sections of two walls a couple of metres left - there is a 'beach' sign on a rock and an arrow pointing along the trail. Our route now continues alongside a stone wall to pass between the ruin of a cottage and a dry well (Wp.4 19M) at the head of the small inlet of **Cala'n Basto** to a trail junction; note the stone boathouse built into the wall of the inlet.

We take the main trail to swing right and walk above **Cala'n Basto** before our route swings (SW) to cross a stone littered plain, some boulders being wind sculpted into almost familiar objects while others have been fused into a glassy surface, to pass the end of a well-kept stone wall (Wp.5 37M).

Beyond the wall it is more of the same as we follow the faint mud streak running across knobbly limestone, the lighthouse coming into view as the streak establishes itself as a rock and dirt path heading generally towards the **Far d'Artrutx** tower. The path runs (S) along the edge of stunted bushes dividing the limestone wasteland from the scrub inland as we start closing with the **Son Olivar** military camp's camouflaged buildings on our front left.

We come to a wall with a gate entrance (Wp.6 51M) and a substantial sign for 'Marina de son Olivaret'. After passing through the gate, our route immediately improves to a dirt trail running through bushes alongside a low stone wall.

We come to a track running through the stone wall on our left (Wp.7 57M) to turn right on the track, which soon reduces to trail width to bring us to the strange sight of a stone slope with a doorway into the slope.

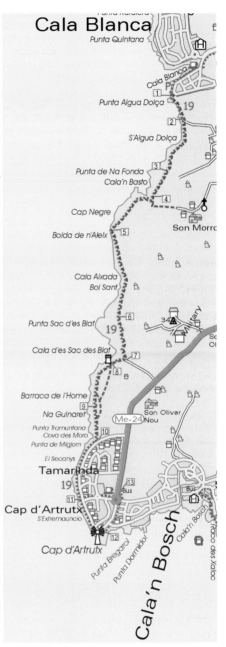

Civil War relics at Wp.8

Following the trail round the slope we find that it is a substantial Civil War gun position (Wp.8); time for exploring the gun position should be added to our route time.

Keeping to the main trail, our route curves to head south and divides, we keep to the seaward path to pass a *talaiot* style construction (Wp.9 69M), before the paths rejoin. Civilisation is ahead as we pass another 'Marina de son Olivaret' sign to go through a gravity gate and come onto pavement at the edge of the resort (Wp.10 76M).

Our finish could not be simpler - a simple stroll along the pavement between the small cliffs and the bungalows on the edge of the urbanisation; these bungalows seeming to hunker down into the rock in an attempt to escape the strong winds. If you are in a rush to finish, then turn left at **Villa Paraiso** (misnamed) (Wp.11 83M) to walk up past the commercials to our finish point. We continue along the pavement to swing inland at the lighthouse (Wp.12), passing the **Paseo Maritimo** on our right before coming up to the roundabout, just beyond which is the bus stop (Wp.13 94M).

This is an easy walk along the spectacular **Galdana** gorge. Stunning scenery, geology, flora and bird life make this route a must for everyone. Virtually flat, you only need to cross a small wall on stepping stones, so lack of fitness is no excuse!

Access by car: There is usually ample parking on the street or on the side of the dirt road.

Access by bus: Routes go to **Cala de Santa Galdana** from **Maó** and **Ciutadella** (some routes require you to change buses in **Ferreries**). See the appendices at the back of this book for details of bus times.

Starting from the roundabout (Wp.1 0M) at the end of the bridge we follow the pavement east and north past the bars and shops until we pass **Galdana Palms** and come onto a dirt road (Wp.2 10M) which takes us up to a pair of metal gates (Wp.3 12M). The stepping stones alongside the gates, half-camouflaged by shrubs and bamboo, allow us pedestrian access.

The 'camouflaged' stepping stones at Wp.3

Over the wall, we continue on the dirt road (NW) to a junction (Wp.4) where we go right to follow the line of the river. Although the gorge is wide, wooded slopes rise up on our left and the air is filled with bird song as we stroll along the dirt road, passing a trail off towards the *torrent* (Wp.5).

Just after our route swings left (Wp.6) we pass a small cave followed by a much larger one on our left (25M). Butterflies flit amongst the wild flowers which line our route, as we come to a trail off to our right (Wp.7 28M), once a crossing over the torrent though the bridge is now broken.

A couple of minutes later we pass through open gates and pass a bridge over the *torrent* (Wp.8 30M). Ahead in the distance, limestone cliffs continue to enclose the *torrent* as our gentle stroll brings us past a stone-built corral (Wp.9 40M).

Now the river bed is choked with bamboo thickets, making for a closed-in feel until we swing left (NW) and the gorge opens up again below superb limestone cliffs (Wp.10 43M).

Having crossed the open area, we come to a cultivated field, fenced with reinforcing mesh (Wp.11) and our broad trail narrows to a single file track. We continue on with bushes pushing in on the route, until we meet the limit of navigation (Wp.12 48M).

We return by retracing our steps through this natural wonderland, finally seeking refreshment in the resort while savouring the memories of this spectacular but easy experience of Menorca.

The beautiful beach of **Cala Macarella** is a popular destination for almost everyone staying in the **Cala de Santa Galdana** resort area. For some unknown reason it is particularly popular to families with pushchairs, despite the steep ascents and descents at each end of the route, although recently it has been improved by the installation of wooden stepped walkways, which make the ascents and descents easier than in the old au-naturel days.

Despite the apparent simplicity of this route, we still find novice walkers heading north towards **Ciutadella** instead of west towards **Cala Macarella**.

2/3   45-55M   2-2½ km   60m / 60m   2*

* at **Bar Suzy**, **Cala Macarella**

Access by car: There is usually space to park on the streets.

Access by bus: Routes go to **Cala de Santa Galdana** from **Maó** and **Ciutadella** (some routes require you to change buses in **Ferreries**). See appendices for details.

Our route starts outside the **Hotel Audax** (Wp.1 0M), a five minute stroll (W & SW) from the roundabout by the bridge. With the new stepped walkway we now have a choice of three options for the first section of our route.

(a) Short and Energetic Route

From the corner opposite the hotel, we go up the stairs, and where the crowds go left over the bridge, we keep straight ahead on a broad path that soon narrows as it climbs amongst the pines overlooking the clear waters of the inlet. The rule is 'onwards and upwards' (SW & W) as we duck under a fallen tree and then climb up through a zigzag. Steady climbing brings us up to a junction (Wp.2 12M) where we come onto a broad trail by a fire warning sign.

(b)&(c) Wooden Stairway and Longer Scenic Route

Continue on the road past **Hotel Audax**, and when the road turns right again, we fork left onto a road which climbs (NW) to come up to the Wooden Stairway on our left, facing a steep flight of concrete stairs on our right.

(b) Wooden Stairway

Stepping off the road, we start climbing the excellent broad stairway that twists up through the trees; it is a magnificent structure but perhaps more wobbly than

The Wooden Stairway

one would expect. At the top of the stair way we come onto a path to go left for an easy stroll round to the Fire sign junction (Wp.2 15M)

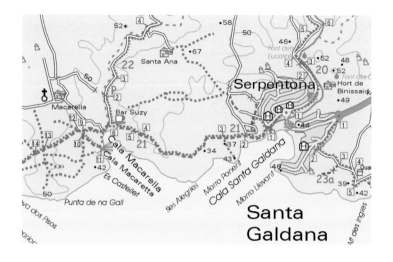

(c)Longer Scenic Route

We continue along the road as it becomes a steeply climbing track, up to a junction of tracks (15M) where we turn left (S) for an easy stroll down to the fire sign junction (Wp.2 23M).

From the junction (0M) we head out (W) on the broad, gladioli-lined trail, passing a walking trail off to our left (Wp.3). Then our route curves left (SW) and the trail splits, left for pushchairs, coming together again after a small rock outcrop. Our wide trail meanders along with very gentle gradients, the direction swinging (SW to NW) until we come to the edge of a deep valley (Wp.4) which runs down to **Cala Macarella**.

We go down into a shallow valley where the broad trail splits (Wp.5), a trail running out to our left a few metres to a viewing point while we start down the second impressive Wooden Stairway to come onto the beach at **Cala Macarella** (Wp.6 30M). Total time ranges from (a) 'Short and Energetic' route (42M) up to (c) 'Longer Scenic' route (53M).

Cala Macarella's Bar Suzy is an archetypal beach bar shaded by trees in contrast to the gleaming white sand of the bay; expect both to be busier than you thought on summer weekends. If you are looking for a quieter cozzie-optional beach, then continue on Walk 24 onto the headland then take the left hand trail (SE) down to the pretty little beach of **Cala Macaretta**.

This is a long country stroll across the western plateau of Menorca to **Ciutadella**. Our ratings assume you follow Walk 21, **Cala de Santa Galdana** to **Cala Macarella** in order to reach our starting point; you will need to add an additional 45 minutes, 2.5 kilometres and 50 metres of ascents and descents to this walk.

3 | 4¾ H | 18½ km | 150m / 150m | 4*

*in **Ciutadella**

Access by car: There is usually space to park on **Cala de Santa Galdana**'s streets.

Access by bus: Routes go to **Cala de Santa Galdana** from **Maó** and **Ciutadella** (some routes require you to change buses in **Ferreries**). See appendices at the back of this book for details.

After our arrival from **Cala de Santa Galdana** we set out from **Bar Suzy** (Wp.1 0M) in **Cala Macarella** - seldom open, unfortunately, before 11 a.m. We follow the dirt road heading inland, going past the vehicle barrier and the meadow car parking area (Wp.2). Past an old water wheel (Wp.3) opposite a spring and where the valley narrows, our route climbs between wooded slopes.

Climbing steadily through the trees, we pass the dirt road entrance to **Santa Ana** (Wp.4 18M) before crossing the stream bed (muddy in wet weather) to climb steeply up from the valley.

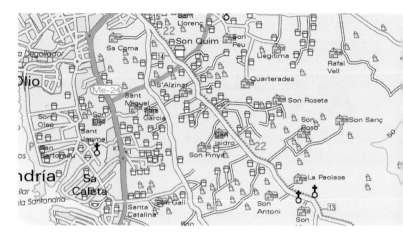

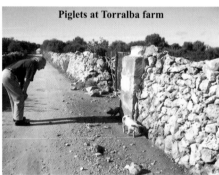

Piglets at Torralba farm

As we climb out of the trees our road changes to rough stone as we stroll past walled meadows, passing **Torralba** farmhouse (Wp.5 40M) where litters of squeaky piglets are often seen running about.

After a few metres, the lane's surface becomes tarmacked (Wp.6) for easy walking, along to **Torralbet** farmhouse (Wp.7), where the lane widens into a country road. Now it is easy strolling through the meadow landscape (NW), passing the dirt road leading to **Bellaventura** on our right (Wp.8) to reach the road junction by **Morvedra Vei** (Wp.9 80M).

Sant Joan de Mises

At the road junction by **Morvedra Vei**, we go left (W) on the narrower lane and stroll past the exclusive **Morvedra Nou Hotel Rural** (Wp.10) and occasional houses, to reach the eastern entrance of **Sant Joan de Mises** (Wp.11 115M). This *ermita* dates from 1287 and celebrates St. John the Baptist's birthday on June 24 with skilled displays of horsemanship.

From the junction at **Sant Joan de Mises** we follow the road (NNW) towards **Ciutadella**, passing an old cross (Wp.12) before coming to a junction (Wp.13 135M) signed left to 'Platges Saura', and back along the way we've come to 'Platja Macarella'.

Following the main road (NW), we pass two old crosses on the right, and soon our route is dotted with houses and house entrances. We stroll through this country/urban landscape to pass the new southern ring road and the notable **Son Quim** cheese factory (Wp.14) shortly before coming to a main junction (Wp.15 170M). Following the main road, we meet the **Ciutadella** ring road at a roundabout.

Across the roundabout, the streets leads us towards the historic heart of the city, with plenty of choices for a well-earned refreshment stops (184M).

23 CALA DE SANTA GALDANA TO CALA MITJANA TO CALA TREBALÚGER + A WOODLAND STROLL

You can drive to **Cala Mitjana** - and many people do - but the walk in from **Cala de Santa Galdana** presents the beautiful bay at its best. Our extension to **Cala Trebalúger** starts with a steep ascent, and finishes with a steep rope-assisted descent, while the centre section is a delightful pinewood stroll. We finish with a woodland stroll on a path that has been created 'accidentally' by people simply looking for an easy woodland stroll, and that's just what it is.

A Cala de Santa Galdana - Cala Mitjana

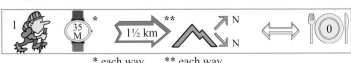

* each way   ** each way

B Cala Mitjana - Cala Trebalúger

* each way   ** each way

C Woodland Stroll

* each way   ** each way

Access by car: Follow the walk description to park in **Plaça Nagran** (Wp.2).
Access by bus: Alight at the first stop, just below the roundabout at the entrance to **Galdana**. (See appendices for timetables)

A Cala de Santa Galdana - Cala Mitjana

From the roundabout at the start of **Galdana** (Wp.1 0M) we take the left hand street to stroll along the pavement between houses and turn into the second cul-de-sac on our left, **Plaça Nagran** and with a 'Cala Mitjana' sign, and cross the car park to a narrow pedestrian entrance, beside locked green gates, in a stone wall (Wp.2 5M). After squeezing through the entrance, we continue on a track through the pines, ignoring a side track off to the right and coming to a gate entrance (Wp.3) where a trail to the right has a line of stones across it. Through the entrance we stay on the track to come to **Cala Mitjana** signs beside a gate entrance (Wp.4 13M).

Following the main track (S) we pass a path and track to a building set just off our route before the track swings left in front of a walled cave (Wp.5 16M). Now we skitter down the track past limestone cliffs to our first views of **Cala Mitjana**, a trail going right to a shelter on the headland. We pass a quarry on

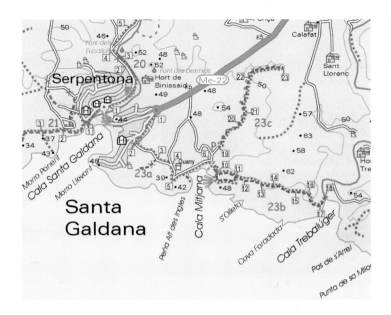

our left, a signboard explaining the cutting of limestone and a path leading into the working area, to walk uphill above the beach followed by gentle downhill to a boardwalk-stair (Wp.6 24M), which accesses the golden sand beach. If you stay on the track you will pass a second boardwalk beach access before reaching the parking area, at the far end of which is the start of our Woodland Stroll.

B Cala Mitjana - Cala Trebalúger

On the eastern side of the beach we step up onto a limestone shelf (Wp.7 0M) to walk seawards for a few metres before turning (Wp.8) to climb steeply up a path onto the headland. It's a hands and feet ascent that brings us panting up amongst the trees (Wp.9 8M) to walk across to a gate in a stone wall (Wp.10 9M). For the main trail to **Cala Trebalúger** you could go left after the gate, but we go right a few metres to stand on the concrete roof of a gun position to take in the best views of **Cala Mitjana**.

Instead of returning to the main trail we follow a path (E) from the gun position, ignoring a path to the right at a junction and following the faint trail through the trees to a large lime kiln and remains of cottages (Wp.11 13M); these remains are easily missed if you are on the main trail. Passing between the two ruins we come onto the main trail, a well manicured official route.

Turning right (E) we have an easy stroll through the pines and brushwood passing a cairned trail off to our right (Wp.12) and a ruin followed by another trail off to our back right (Wp.13). We pass another trail, and lime kiln, on our right just before a trail to the left (Wp.14); rocks across the lefthand trail indicating no route while green paint blobs confirm the official route. Through a stone wall our trail runs gently downhill to emerge from the trees at the edge of an abandoned field (Wp.15).

After skirting the field our trail comes back amongst the trees, narrowing to a path as it threads its way through the trees and a stone wall (Wp.16). Stones in the path's surface are well worn by walkers' boots as we start to descend, green dots confirming the manicured official route, to views through the trees to **Cala Trebalúger**.

Cala Trebalúger

Now it is steeply down on a semi-stepped descent, a fallen pine making a good vantage seat (Wp.17) before dropping down to emerge from the trees onto a limestone outcrop above the beach (Wp.18 36M).

Our final scramble down the outcrop is assisted by a pair of ropes (check that they are securely anchored to the trees before using them) for us to drop onto this pristine beach a 'million miles' from the tourist hordes. We return by the same route, except that this time we stay on the official trail all the way to the gate (Wp.10), and take particular care on the descent to **Cala Mitjana**.

C Woodland Stroll

On our search for the elusive **Camí de Cavalls** we came on this well-walked path which seemed to be heading in the right direction. It did not work out, finally petering out at a large stone barrage wall deep in a wooded valley; the path being made well-walked by the number of people like us simply wandering to the end of navigation and returning. There is little point to this route except that it is a pretty wooded valley/gorge with plenty of shade if you would like a break from the beach.

Our start is at the NE corner of the large car parking area, where we find a track leading (NE) into the trees (Wp.19 0M). In a few metres the track narrows to a trail leading us through the woods, our path skirting a fallen pine (Wp.20) and passing some solid stonework before coming to the first of the stonewall-barrages (Wp.21 8M); these barrages are a feature of the valley dating back to when these sections were agricultural plots. Pushing through the foliage, secatuers useful, the tree cover intensifies and after squeezing under a fallen pine we come below limestone cliffs (Wp.22 17M). Following a cave and limestone pinnacle, we encounter a larger barrage wall and fallen pines before we reach the end of navigation at a very substantial barrage wall (Wp.23 32M); there is a path off to the left just before this point but it only leads up to cultivated fields. We return to the parking area by retracing our steps.

Cala de Santa Galdana to **Cala'n Bosch** is the big hike in south-west Menorca, taking in the beautiful beaches of **Cala Macarella**, **Cala Turqueta**, **Cala Talaier**, and **Platja de Son Saurer** before arriving at the resort beach of **Platja Son Xoriguer**. A large stone wall has cut our original route, so now we follow the coastal path around the **Talaia d'Artrutx**. For the very energetic, walking the route out and return will certainly build up an appetite for dinner.

Access by bus: Routes go to **Cala de Santa Galdana** from **Maó** and **Ciutadella** (some routes require you to change buses in **Ferreries**). See appendices for details.

Short Walk Option

Walk 21 to **Cala Macarella** and return. Follow our walk 'Cala Galdana to Cala Macarella' as far as **Bar Suzy** at **Cala Macarella** (Wp.6 53M).

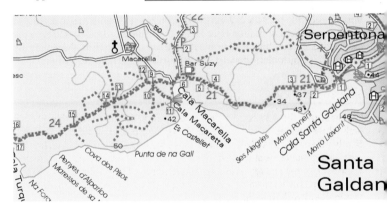

Leaving **Cala Macarella** (0M), we cross the beach (W) to go over a water culvert and come to a junction of paths; a walking trail on our left leads to cave houses, while the gated dirt road heads uphill to locked gates outside the **Macarella** farmhouse. We take the third trail, waymarked with a green arrow, to climb up through the trees (W) to pass through a wall (Wp.7). Our gradient eases, and shortly after a narrow trail goes off to our left (Wp.8) before we come onto a broad walking trail (Wp.9 6M) at a T-junction.

Here we take a short diversion, by going south-east and passing a trail (Wp.10) which drops down into the tiny bay of **Macaretta**, to come onto the headland (Wp.11) for impressive views into the bays of **Macarella** and **Macaretta**.

Back at the T-junction, we follow the wide trail (NW) to a gate entrance (Wp.12 20M), where we go left (WSW) alongside a wall which crosses the head of the **Macaretta** valley. We come to a crossroads of paths (Wp.13) and continue straight ahead through small pines to pass through a wall (Wp.14).

Our path heads through open scrubland towards a tower, the **Talaia d'Artrutx**, and we come to a junction by a stone wall (Wp.15).

Looking back to Cala Turqueta

We go through the wall and drop into a shallow valley to walk through woodland (SW & W) the *talaia* closer each time it comes into view. After passing an old stone-cutting area on our left, we swing into the **Turqueta** valley (Wp.16 50M) to emerge by the water wheel at the seaward end of the parking area (€5 per car).

Our original route from **Cala Turqueta** climbed up to the **Talaia d'Atrutx** but this route has now been closed off by a large stone wall, so we now have a coastal route to **Cala Talaier**.

From **Turqueta** beach (Wp.17) we climb up a steep path marked by a red arrow beside a stone hut, to push through bushes and come over a crest; this brings us above the second inlet and a boat house, and onto a clear path (Wp.18). Our trail swings right (inland) where we take the first or second path on our left - they meet again (Wp.19) to form a well walked trail (S) which we follow up to the wall (Wp.20). Here our trail swings left for us to pass a path signed 'no passar' on our right (Wp.21) as we head through the low scrub to curve around above the coast and come back to the wall (Wp.22) and step onto a track used in the wall's construction. Heading down the track, alongside the wall, we come past a sign board (empty) (Wp.23 85M) to step onto the beach path running through the pines to **Talaier** beach

After crossing the back of the beach, we head south-west (SW) between gateposts (Wp.24), and keep right at a junction (Wp.25) to pass a bunker on our left. There are various tracks amongst the dunes and scrub though we keep WNW between the beach and the wetlands to come to old gun positions which overlook the beach (Wp.26 100M) of **Platja Son Saurer**.

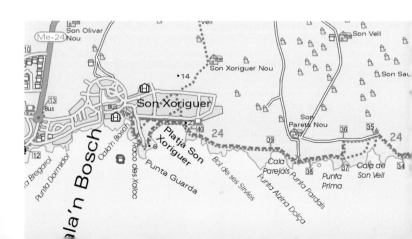

Many writers praise the cozzie-optional bay of **San Saurer** for its lack of development, but in our opinion it would be much improved by the addition of one small structure - a *tipico* beach bar!

After enjoying the near-idyllic **Son Saurer** bay, we head off towards **Cala'n Bosch** (0M). At the western end of the beach (Wp.27) we meet a dirt road and take the walking trail (WSW), to pass another trail on our right before going through a gate in a stone wall (Wp.28). We keep straight ahead when the trail splits (8M) and go past another path on our right, before passing another gun position overlooking the bay (Wp.29). Keeping to the main path, we curve round (W) to overlook the azure waters of the inlet beside **Punta Barraqueta** (Wp.30 14M). We cross the head of the inlet to keep west over rocky, open ground to another gun position (Wp.31 20M) at a junction, where we go left through an old wall. Following the trail, we cross the head of an inlet (Wp.32) to keep west (W) above the cliffs on the faint trail. We pass between caves dug either side of the trail (Wp.33 33M) before meeting a steel gate (Wp.34 35M).

Once through the gate, we follow the track which widens to a dirt road (Wp.35 44M) as we pass through a wall and a track off to our left. We come to a machine gun post at a gate entrance (Wp.36) where we take a trail to our left (S). We go south and then turn right (W) at a junction (Wp.37) to walk alongside a recently built stone wall. After passing through a gate (Wp.38 57M), we get our first views of **Cala'n Bosch** as we pass a private entry to **Son Parets Nou** on our right and a hut on our left, followed by a stone-built gun emplacement (Wp.39 64M).

We come level with the development of **Son Xoriguer** inland of us as the broad trail curves WNW for us to walk alongside the bay of **Son Xoriguer**. Our final section into **Cala'n Bosch** is easy to follow, as we take the path around **Platja Son Xoriguer** and out onto **Punta Guarda** which then heads north-west (NW) past **Cala'n Bosch** bay and to the bus stop opposite the hotel. However, after seventy-five minutes of walking from **San Saura**, the sight of the welcoming bars to the north of us (Wp.40) is too much of a temptation. We take a small path across to the **King Kong** and **Miramar** bars after well over three hours of non-stop walking from our start at **Cala de Santa Galdana** (228M), to substantially increase the island's beverage sales before tackling the final short stage to the bus stop (Wp.41).

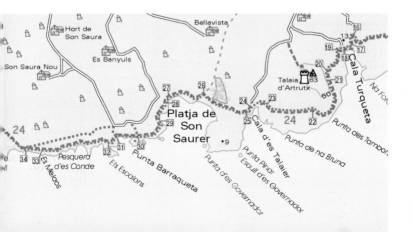

What begins as a country stroll from one of Menorca's important archaeological sites becomes a surprising adventure into some more recent history. Take refreshments with you in order to take time exploring **Lluc al Lari**. Originally this was a figure of eight route down the country track to **Sant Llorenç** farm, but so popular did this new route become that the owner has now locked the gates due to the volumes of walkers; please respect their privacy. The closure might have more to do with the hippies at **Lluc al Lari** being granted resident voting rights by the town hall, much against the wishes of local land owners. If you do have any problems with the hippies, very unlikely, do report the problem to your hotel and the police.

Once you could drive to **Lluc al Lari** but now the *pistacia* bushes have pushed onto the tarmac lane so much you risk serious bodywork damage, and substantial surcharge on your credit card, if you try driving to the fort in your hire car.

*panhandle linear

Poblat Torre d'en Galmés

We start from the **Poblat Torre d'en Galmés** which is reached on the tarmac lane signed off the **Sant Jaume** road, approximately 2.5 kilometres south of **Alaior**. We park in the *poblat*, (Wp.1 0M), exploring this extensive historic site before heading south on the continuation of the tarmac lane.

Torre d'en Galmés (also known as Torre d'en Gaumes) is now a pay site for visitors, so if you prefer not to make payment for parking fork right at the junction (Wp.2) and park alongside the lane before it narrows after the entrance to **Santa Cecilia** (Wp.3).

From **Torre d'en Galmés** (Wp.1 0M) we walk back down the road to the junction (Wp.2 6M) to go left for a bucolic stroll along the deteriorating lane to pass the entrance (Wp.3 11M) up to **Santa Cecilia**. If you are wondering why we are walking this quiet lane, instead of driving slowly round the potholes, the next few minutes should convince you as the *pistacia* bushes start enclosing our route and the potholes become more noticeable; these are some of the most vigorous bushes on the island and have the same effect as bears claws if you try to drive past them at speed. Gradually the bushes reduce the roadway to below car width, unfortunately also obscuring the views but we can look out for the wild tortoises frequently seen on this route. Slight curves in the lane restrict the view ahead, rather like a bush filled gully, so a well in the field on our left (Wp.4) and views across to **Sant Llorenç** farm (Wp.5) are welcome features before we come to a dirt track crossing the

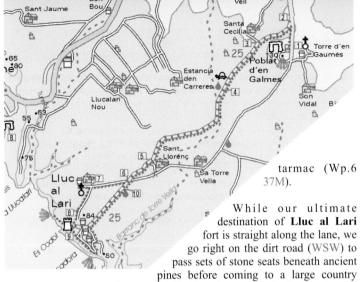

tarmac (Wp.6 37M).

While our ultimate destination of **Lluc al Lari** fort is straight along the lane, we go right on the dirt road (WSW) to pass sets of stone seats beneath ancient pines before coming to a large country mansion (Wp.7 41M). The mansion was once the quarters for the commander of the coastal fort but has been abandoned and sadly vandalised for some time. Staff quarters and a chapel still stand in its grounds, and the remains of an ornamental garden struggle to maintain some dignity.

From the mansion we head south on an overgrown dirt road which crosses the head of a valley running down to the sea on our right. Coming up from the valley, we pass between large gate posts (Wp.8) before the dirt road peters out and buildings come into sight. Passing a circular observation post (Wp.9 45M) we enter the former **Lluc al Lari** military camp. Across the open ground, we strike the tarmac lane which comes from **Torre d'en Galmés**, and our attention is grabbed by the amazing sight of a huge military gun - and not just one gun, as there's a second fifty metres to our right! The underground control rooms for the guns are welded shut, preventing budding militarists from triggering a bombardment, but otherwise this military camp is largely intact. Observation and range-finding positions built into the top of the cliffs offer superb coastal views, these cliff top positions stretching almost a kilometre to the south-east; if you have an interest in twentieth century military, allow plenty of time to explore this largest of Menorca's coastal forts. Unfortunately perhaps, the old camp has been hippified and the huge guns decorated as pop-art take away the brooding air that used to hang over the camp when it was deserted. A dirt road brings us back to the entrance to the base.

Our return (0M) retraces our easy stroll along the tarmac lane, usually traffic free except for the occasional hippy. *Pistacia* bushes immediately start pushing in on the lane as we pass a well on our right (Wp.10) before coming to the crossroads of our outward route (Wp.6 8M). The views ahead are dominated by **Mount Toro** and **Poblat d'en Galmés** as we stroll past **Sant Llorenç** (Wp.5) with its large threshing circles. A gentle downhill section takes us past another well (Wp.4 30M) and then it is gently uphill between cultivated fields to pass the entrance to **Santa Cecilia** (Wp.3) with **Poblat d'en Galmés** looming over us on our right. Unfortunately, there is no short cut to the *poblat* so we stroll up to the junction of the lane (Wp.2 40M) and then head south to come back to our start point (Wp.1), 45 minutes from the guns.

26 SANT TOMÁS - SON BOU

This popular route between **Sant Tomás** and **Son Bou** looks easy on a map, but much of the walk is on soft sand, making it much tougher than it looks. Also, it is best to avoid windy days when the blowing sand can make the dunes a survival exercise.

Access by bus: There are bus routes to **Sant Tomás** (you may find it called Cala Tomás at the bus station) from **Maó** and from **Ciutadella**. (See appendices for details.)

Access by car: Park in the large car park at the eastern end of **Sant Tomás** and walk down to our start.

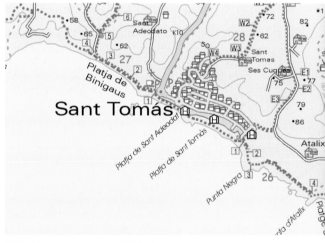

Platja de Binigaus at Sant Tomás.

We start out from below **Hotel Victoria**, by the signboard, 'Platja d'Atalitx 25M, Platja Son Bou 1H' (Wp.1 0M) to climb up from the beach (SE) past a cave and onto **Punta Negra**. This rocky area (Wp.2) has no formal paths, so we keep heading SSE to come across the headland.

Ahead, **Son Bou** comes into view (Wp.3) while closer to hand, pimples of rock puncture the azure sea along the rugged coastline. Inland, meadows ablaze with wild flowers run up to the edge of pine woods as we come onto a better defined coastal path (SE).

We begin to pass tiny bays on our right with the **Atalix** country estate inland of us, as we stroll along to a bridge (Wp.4 15M) over the **Torrent Son Boter** which runs into its impressive bay. Across the bridge, the idyllic little beach of **Platja d'Atalitx** is on our right, as we walk along to pass through a gate (Wp.5) and drop down to the start of **Platjes de Son Bou**.

We are now into serious beach and sand dune territory, with our destination of **San Bou** still over two kilometres away. Our choice is between the soft sand beach, the slighter firmer damp sand along the sea's edge, or the low, grassy sand dunes. Whichever option we choose, it is still a slog - far tougher than it appears on a map. On our left, the lagoon and wetlands of **Sant Jaume**, edged with reeds and bamboo thickets, form a boundary to the dunes. We head SE past an island, sculpted by erosion into the image of a cruising ship. Gradually, the 'cozzie optional' nature of the beach gives way to family groups as we come down to the lagoon's outlet into the sea (Wp.6 40M) which flows only as a narrow stream except after heavy rain.

Across the outlet, we come onto a fully commercial beach with opportunities for refreshments and beach or sea activities. We can leave the beach on a sand road (Wp.7 45M) though our logical route is to continue past the **Milanos** and **Pinguinos** hotels to the walled-in *basilica* (the remains of an early Christian church) at the end of the beach (Wp.8 55M). Don't expect too many distractions in the pocket resort of **Son Bou** before your return to **Sant Tomás** - and nearly three kilometres of soft sand before reaching the solid ground after **Platja d'Atalitx**!

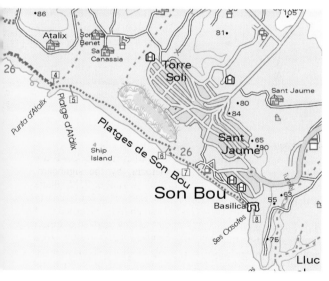

This interesting walk takes in a coastal path, a climb on a donkey trail up through a lush valley, along with Menorca's most impressive and best known caves.

3   2H   7½ km   130m / 130m   ↻ *   2**

* panhandle circular
** at start and end

Access by Bus: Routes from both **Maó** and **Ciutadella** run to **Sant Tomás**. See appendices for details.

Access by Car: As we arrive at the seafront roundabout, turn right into the large car park behind the Bar/Restaurant.

Taking the path around the front of the bar (Wp.1 0M) we head westwards along the coast. Our narrow path follows the coastline, passing an old pillbox (now used as a boat hut) on our right and islands on our left, to come to the start of the **Binigaus** beach (Wp.2). It's reasonably easy walking until our path drops onto the beach (Wp.3 10M), where we have to slog across the soft sand towards old pillboxes, then swinging right to come onto a dirt road (Wp.4) by a shanty; which proves to be a jovial Spanish pensioner's sculpture workshop.

The trail at Wp.14

Now it is easy walking along the dirt road (N) through the shallow valley until we pass through a gate (Wp.5 20M) where a sign directs us onto a walking trail. Over a wall on stepping stones, our narrow trail curves round from east to north as we cross small fields before crossing another wall (Wp.6).

Now the trail cuts across the tree-covered, sloping valley side (N) where there is little sign of human habitation except for the squared-off stones on the left side of the path. Pruners would be useful as bushes push in on our path - beware of occasional thorns - until we zigzag up through a wall to come onto a cobbled donkey trail (Wp.7) and a junction.

The right hand path leads across the valley floor to **Cova des Coloms** (not signed), one of the huge caves for which this valley is famous. Back at the junction, we continue on the main path in a gentle ascent, crossing another wall (Wp.8 50M), with the landscape becoming gentler as we approach the valley's upper reaches. At another wall (Wp.9), a small path goes right to more caves while we continue (N) on the main path, keeping left when the path forks.

At the next junction (Wp.10) we go left, ascending the valley wall, and then the trail levels out and we come to a signed junction; '5 minutes to the caves' (Wp.11 60M). We take the steep path down to cross the valley floor for a steady climb up through zigzags to the cave entrance (Wp.12 65M). Through a defile, we come into the cathedral-sized cave. Despite its dimensions, the cave is well lit at floor level, while bats squeak high up on the dark, cavernous roof.

Back at the junction (Wp.11 0M) on the west side of the valley, we continue inland (N) on the path, which becomes boulder-laid and climbs steadily to pass through a wall (Wp.13). Steady climbing brings us up and out of the valley and onto a plateau where we stroll over to a signboard beside a dirt road (Wp.14 10M). Our route is left (SW), though going right would take you to **Es Migjorn Gran** in 20 minutes of walking; see extension.

After the climb up and out of the valley, our return is an easy stroll (SW) down past a well and then through a gated entrance (Wp.15 15M) as views open up over the valley to our right. A gentle uphill section takes us past another well before strolling down to pass through the gates of **Binigaus Nou** (Wp.16). Passing in front of the house, we go through another set of gates, and our trail starts to drop down into the valley past another well. Our route zigzags down to the valley floor and heads seawards (SW), curving south for us to pass through a gated entrance (Wp.17), and then along to join our outward route by the signboard (Wp.5 38M). From here, we retrace our outward route to arrive back on the bar terrace (Wp.1 60M).

Extension to Es Migjorn Gran

Coming onto the dirt road (Wp.14 0M) we go right (NE) up the track to pass the entrance lane to **Binigaus Vell** (Wp.18). Our track undulates along gradually climbing to pass another farm entrance lane (Wp.19) and **Sa Vinya des Metge Camps** to come over a crest. An abandoned *talaiot* is passed as we stroll along to the cemetery junction (Wp.20 15M) to join the route of Walk 28. To finish in **Es Migjorn Gran** we continue ahead, passing the town's 'official' *talaiot* to the **Francesc Dalbranca** school (Wp.21 18M). From here we can either go right down to the **Sant Tomás** road, or ahead through the town streets to the roundabout bus stop.

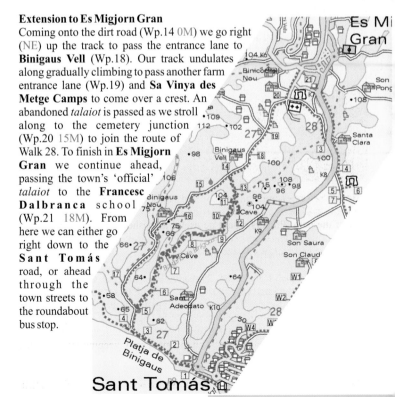

If you are staying in **Sant Tomás** and looking for an easy stroll to work up an appetite for dinner, then this pair of routes gives you a choice of which end of the resort you wish to finish at. Those less fortunate can still enjoy this route either as a linear country stroll or combined with Walk 27 as a more energetic circular.

Access by bus: to **Es Migjorn Gran** or **Sant Tomás**

Access by car: park in **Es Migjorn Gran** near the sports ground (see map).

Short Circular Walk
Select either the Alternative Finish in reverse up to Wp.8 and then return to **Sant Tomás** by the other route.

From the **Es Migjorn Gran** bus stop at the roundabout we have a choice of starts. Quickest is to walk back down the main road to meet our official route (Wp.3 7M) but far more scenic is our 'official' route of walking up the town's main shopping street and working our way through to the **Francesca Dalbranca** school (Wp.1 0M).

We head south past the town's offical *talaiot* to the cemetery junction (Wp2 3M) where we go left down a walled track running through pretty countryside past a pair of circular *embalses* into a shallow valley, from where we climb up to the **Sant Tomás** 'main' road (Wp.3 12M). Crossing the road to the **Santa**

Clara entrance, we head uphill to a junction (Wp.4 17M) signed 'Depuradura'; meaning 'rubbish' but don't be dismayed by this inauspicious start.

Leaving the 'main' road behind we stroll out along the track with views down to the coast to come to the **Santa Mónica** *talaiot* (Wp.5) on the left of our track; a quick climb over the stone wall (official access) gives access to explore the historic site (Wp.6). Back on the track we pass the pretty **Santa Mónica** farmhouse (Wp.7 25M) on our left and the entrance to **Son Saura** on our right. The new Depuradura water treatment works come into view ahead as we pass **Son Barber** and our track runs downhill to the the works artificial pool (clear!) and then undulates along to a junction (Wp.8 37M).

Alternative Finish West

Going right at the junction we follow the track across a shallow valley to a trio of gates (Wp.W1). Through the centre gates (leave them as you find them) we come into a wooded area for a gentle downhill stroll through a gate entrance and passing a *talaiotic* stone mound (Wp.W2) before coming out of the woodland between a pair of 'sentinel' pines to stroll down to the **Sant Tomás** farm (Wp.W3 48M). At the farmyard we turn right to leave on a dirt track, the first of the resort's developments coming into view as we come along to join a tarmac road by **Casa Es Migjorn** and **Sa Punta** (Wp.W4).

The stone mound at Wp.W2

Now we head down the street to a junction where the rule is 'always head downhill'. Going right we head steeply downhill to pass a traffic island (Wp.W5) by **Villa Ana**, where we go right and then left past a second traffic island to continue downhill to emerge on the resort's main road opposite the **Sol Menorca Hotel** (Wp.W6 61M).

Alternative Finish East

Here the main track swings right but we keep straight ahead on a rough cobbled track (S) passing **Binicodrell de Baix** farm to run gently downhill, followed by gently uphill to a concrete barn (Wp.E1 44M). Now the track gets much rougher as it runs downhill past a walking trail (Wp.E2) on our left for us to come to a set of gates (Wp.E3 49M). Past the gates we continue on the rough track to a junction where we take a trail heading west which runs into the eastern end of the resort.

Cales Coves is a spectacular inlet edged with limestone cliffs which also houses one of the largest groups of talaiotic necropolis burial caves in the Balearics. Theoretically, you can drive down the stone track from above **Son Vitamina**, but many visitors baulk at seeing the rough track that runs down to a small, and packed at weekends, parking area behind the beach, so our description assumes you park at the start of the track. Personally, we drive the track but it is a most vibratory experience that possibly breaches your hire car contract.

An alternative **B Route** in from the edge of **Cala en Porter** provides a shorter access route from a tarmac road, or as a route out of the resort itself.

Technically the Circular route is a one hour walk from the parking area, but there is so much to look at that normal walking times do not really apply. You can choose to investigate the necropolis caves on the south of the inlet, but bear in mind that this is scrambling and narrow ledge country, not easy walking.

N.B. If walking from the beginning of the track at **Son Vitamina**, add 1 Hour, 4.5 kilometres and 70 metres of gentle Ascents/Descents.

From Son Vitamina to Cales Coves Beach

From the large tarmac circle just off the ME-12 at the start of **Son Vitamina** we set off down the track (Wp.1 0M) for an easy stroll past the large farm of **Biniedrix de Dalt** (right) and a bungalow (left); the track far more comfortable as an easy stroll than a 'shaken and stirred' drive. Gradually the track runs downhill for us to go through a metal gate (Wp.2 19M) after which our route runs down into a valley to pass below a large house shortly before the track runs out at a small parking area at the back of the beach (Wp.3 26M).

From Cales Coves Beach

Solita 1910

Going to the right of the beach, we come onto the rocks by a boathouse to find steps (Wp.4 0M) and a red arrow directing us on a rock path around the headland. A second red arrow keeps us on the occasionally stepped path as we curve round the headland onto the inland arm of **Cales Coves**. Past our first cave (locked) and a great fissure of limestone we come below **Solita 1910**; surely the most isolated country house on the island. Keeping to the main path - more arrows for guidance - brings us past an open cave to a junction (Wp.5 7M) where the 'playa' is signed left.

Keeping to the main path, signed 'mirador', we start climbing quite seriously to pass more caves; mostly barred since the official eviction of their hippy occupants. Our steady climb on the good trail brings us up to the *mirador* viewpoint (Wp.6 13M). After taking in the impressive views of the *cala* - actually all the views are pretty impressive but this is probably the most impressive - we continue uphill to pass through an entry in a stone wall and keeping to the main trail the gradient moderates for us to stroll up to a 'Cala en Porter' sign on a rock (Wp.7 18M) as we come onto a track leading up to locked gates ahead of us.

Following the sign we stroll along the left arm of the track, curving gently downhill and cutting off a loop of the track on a walking trail, and coming down to cross the floor of a valley and pass through another substantial stone wall (Wp.8 25M). What goes down must come up as we start ascending the southern side of the valley, views opening up to reward our effort, until we come to the crest beside an old well (Wp.9 34M); well (sic) worth looking at for its own sake as well as a break after the climb. Shortly after the well trails head off through the bush towards **Cala en Porter** and when our track swings left (Wp.10 37M) another trail continues ahead into the bush.

We have an easy stroll along the track to a path junction (Wp.11 40M). On a rock set in the north side of the track is an old scratched arrow pointing down a path; this is the path described in Dodo Mackenzie's route but now so overgrown as to be dangerously impassable; our own waymark now directs walkers in the correct direction.

Continuing (E) we stroll along the track, narrowing to a trail as it passes through a substantial stone wall for us to come to a path junction amongst the pines marked by a small cairn (Wp.12 44M); it is important that you do not miss this junction. Going left on the minor path we come to the edge of the gorge where a narrow rock path is the start of our exciting descent; GPS reception is soon lost after this point, so put the unit away and concentrate on the descent.

Our narrow cliff-face path needs concentration so take care with each step, a slow descent is preferable to a disastrous 'fast' drop; in the mornings before the sun has dried this north facing cliff, the rocks can be slippery with dew. There is only one way down, and rocky zig-zags giving way to dirt and bushes. Given the nature of the descent, it's a surprise when it suddenly stops as we come to a T-junction beside a watercourse (55M). Left leads to the blocked Dodo route, so we turn right to push through the bushes and pass a cave on our right before coming to the little beach at the head of **Cales Coves'** inland arm (58M). Following a path from the tiny beach beside a wall we come to a clamber up onto a red arrowed trail which climbs up to join our outward route (Wp.5 63M), from where we retrace our steps back to the main beach.

29 B Route: Cales Coves start from Cala en Porter

This exciting short walk offers the option to turn the route into a larger circular by incorporating our main route. Ideal if you are looking to escape the 'resort' atmosphere of **Cala en Porter**.

In **Cala en Porter** we start on the eastern side of the resort/urbanisation. If driving keep left to come onto the long straight street dividing the housing from the wild countryside, **Carrer de Sant Domenec**. As you drive down the street, look for a white painted pedestrian entrance in the wall on your left (E) and park nearby.

From the white pedestrian entrance (Wp.B1 0M) we follow a dirt path through the bushes and pines. Almost immediately we are at our first path junction, and our first problem in describing this route; the whole plateau above the limestone cliffs is a network of little paths. In this rather featureless terrain we simply try to follow what we see as the main path while keeping to an approximately east-southeast direction inland of the cliffs. Our paths are a mixture of dirt, rock litter and limestone as we come to round the seaward end of a stone wall (Wp.B2 3M). Continuing on the main path (or what appears to be the main path), the only way to replicate a route through this bushland is with gps track navigation. Coming to a stone cairn (Wp.B3 6M) we curve left (E-ENE) to pass inland of a limestone outcrop (Wp.B4), our path becoming more defined for us to come onto a track (Wp.11 10M) to join our main route.

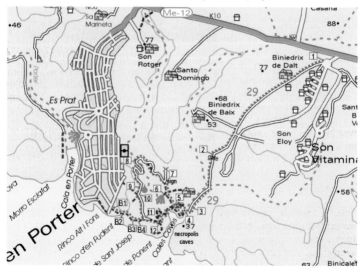

Castell de Santa Agueda was the site of the Moors' last stand in Menorca in 1287 against King Alfonso. While no trace of the castle remains, this short ascent does reward us with atmospheric views from this historic site.

Access by car: Turn off the **Ciutadella - Ferreries** ME-1 road onto the **Camí des Alocs** road, and drive north until reaching the modernist but abandoned school house by the gated entrance to **Santa Cecilia**. There is space for four or five cars to park, but take care not to block the road or entrance.

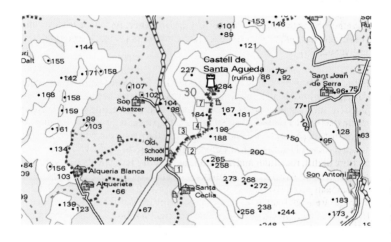

We follow the track alongside the right side of the schoolhouse (Wp.1 0M), going uphill through the metal gates. Water erosion has removed the stone surface on this lower part of the route, leading to muddiness in wet weather, but in a couple of minutes we come onto the remains of boulder-laid sections as we climb up between trees (NE).

The start of the route

Passing through a stone wall (Wp.2 5M), we continue upwards through denser trees, the surface of this Roman road improving as it gains height. Our route swings ENE (Wp.3 8M) on its relentless upward march, then gradually swings back towards the north to come alongside an old stone wall (Wp.4 12M) for us to come onto the original stone-laid surface of the path.

The path ahead appears to be blocked off, though a dirt path swings right (E) before climbing through a hairpin bend (Wp.5) to pass a field entrance on our right and come through a gate and back onto the old stone-laid trail (Wp.6 17M); the adventurous can cut off this dirt path section by continuing on the stone-laid path and scrambling up the boulders and onto the path's continuation by the gate.

As we climb steadily alongside the wall (N), views across the northern landscapes open up, and we come to a shed on our right (Wp.7 22M) and the more surprising sight of a 1930's car rusting away beside our trail. Now we are climbing seriously (N) to reach a section of zigzags (Wps 8, 9 & 10). The bends make good rest points from which to admire what remains of the castle walls before we tackle the final slopes up to the abandoned farm buildings which occupy this historic site (Wp.11 30M).

On Santa Agueda's trig point

Although virtually nothing remains of the old castle, from the plateau on the peak we enjoy spectacular views before returning by the same route down to our car.

West of **Ferreries** is a most unusual walk up the weathered fissure in a limestone gorge, only short but completely unique amongst Menorca's walking routes. We have combined this unusual route with an easy stroll into the **Galdana** gorge to provide a different view of the countryside.

Intrepid hire car drivers can drive the very narrow *camino rural* and then rough dirt track to the parking area above **Es Canato** hostel, though we recommend parking at the cemetery west of **Ferreries** and stretching your legs along the country lane.

3 | 3 H | 10½ km | 200m / 200m | * | 0

* panhandle circular

Access by bus: The **Maó - Ciutadella - Maó** and **Maó - Cala Galdana** routes stop at **Ferreries**. See appendices for details.

Access by car: park at the **Ferreries** cemetery on the western edge of the town.

Short Route
In total this is a panhandle circular, though you can leave off the panhandle by taking the **Camí Reial** from Wp.8 for an interesting circular route but without the unique features of the full route. (2 hours. 7.5 kilometres Ascents/Descents 120 metres.)

We start out from the cemetery (Wp.1 0M), with the unappetising prospect of crossing over and walking along the main ME-1 road (W) past the **Santa Galdana** road. Coming steadily uphill we pass the entrance to **Biniatrum** to swing left (Wp.2 5M) and climb up a narrow tarmac lane away from the main road.

Ferreries cemetery

A steady climb is rewarded with views over the ME-1 and Menorca's western plain as we stroll along the *camino rural*, swinging towards the west and running down to cross a shallow valley. Climbing up from the valley floor our views are to the south as we pass the gated entrance to **Son Gomés** as the lane continues ascending past a cottage (Wp.3 22M).

As our lane swings south (Wp.4 29M) the trees clear by a low stone wall to give views over the northern valley. It is more of the same as we stroll south through the tranquil countryside accompanied by distant views over the southern landscapes; passing the gated entrance of **Son Bell-lloquet** (Wp.5), a track running out between stone walls (Wp.6) to **Sant Joan**, and **Na**

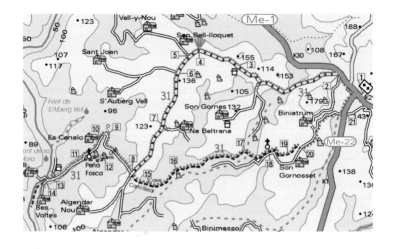

Beltrana's entrance (Wp.7) before coming to face the locked gates of **Algendar Nou** (Wp.8 51M) and a junction with a 'Camí Reial' on the left and a dirt track dropping down to our right.

Taking the track (NW) we head down to cross a cattle grid into meadows and over a small rise we stroll down to a grass parking area (Wp.9, 66M) just before the track is barred to vehicle traffic; unless the track has been graded you will now realise why we recommend walking to this point rather than risking an excess claim for damage on your hire car contract.

Past the vehicle barrier, our track starts dropping into the **Algendar** gorge to pass the **Es Canato** hostel (Wp.10) with its interesting waterwheel; and possibly interesting refreshments if they are open. We drop down the track beneath limestone cliffs as the gorge develops around us, plots of abandoned fruit trees lining the floor of the gorge, and we come down to a large stone cross set on a rock outcrop and the unusual sign of 'Es Pasten Riddle y Pena Fosca' beside a steel ladder dropping into a water runoff (Wp.11 73M).

Now we step off the track (0M) to descend the ladder into the water runoff to start walking up into a green moss region, feeling like a haunted alleyway with plant tendrils reaching for us; secateurs useful. After a short clear section we encounter sawn logs and a tree growing in the limestone fissure, the sheer walls seeming to suffer from 'rock worm' as we climb up the defile. When another fissure goes off to our right behind a large tree we continue ahead towards a wall to climb up to the substantial remains of a house built in the fissure; set deep in the cutting it would perhaps suit someone allergic to direct sunlight - eerie.

From the house a plant clogged path continues up the ravine, and crossing the water course we come up through a gap in the dense foliage to climb over a stone wall into the open air. Continuing up to the top of the outcrop (Wp.12 13M; note there is no GPS reception between Wps. 11&12) we find ourselves in an area of fields, stone walls and bushes. A faint path runs through the bushes to pass large caves once used as houses, a more substantial cave house sits at the end of the outcrop just before a stone water trough and cistern. There is no official way out of this intriguing area, except to plunge back down the route of our ascent giving us time to marvel at the house and water sculpted limestone before climbing up the steel ladder to the bemused stares of unknowing visitors to the **Algendar** gorge.

Continuing down the gorge we have an easy stroll down the track to pass the locked gates of a farm on our right (Wp.13) before coming to where our gorge joins the main **Algendar** gorge beside the entrance to **Ses Voltes** (Wp.14). After the confines of the minor gorge we are now in a much wider, wetter and airier region and it is rather surprising after the lack of habitation to this point to find substantial houses clustered in this region. It is possible to wander a little further down the main gorge before the water and cliffs close off the route or until we head back. It's a steady, possibly slogging, ascent back up to **Es Canato**, which makes a pleasant half way stopping place (even more pleasant if it's open for refreshments) in the climb back up out of the gorge and up to the 'Camí Reial' junction.

For our return, or if taking the Short Route option, we take the **Camí Reial** (0M **Ferreries** 3.5km) to come down the narrow trail to 'Portel de Algendar' and 'Sa Costa de na Salina' signs (Wp.15 3M) followed by a cave named **Sa Cova Reial**, the signs all done with some artistic flourish. A limestone cutting makes a natural seating area, a good rest point if walking the route in reverse, before we come down to an abandoned cottage 'Es Pou de Sa Perdue Blanca' (Wp.16) where the remains of a water aqueduct still run alongside our trail before crossing the valley on our right.

The 'Costa de na Salina' sign

The trail is now a pleasant undulating stroll but with few views through the trees as we pass through a gate entrance and then a second gate entrance (Wp.17 20M) into a valley. We go down to cross the valley floor to start a steady twisting ascent up through the trees and stone walls, the ascent becoming gentler after the first climb as we come up to a cross, **Sa Crue de Son Gornes** dated 1865 (Wp.18). Our trail swings right and runs downhill to cross another valley floor followed by a steady climb past a tiny garden apparently dedicated to 'Oscar' (Wp.19) before we come up to join a dirt track beside the entrance to **Son Gornosset** (Wp.20 38M).

Turning left we stroll along the track to pass industrial farm buildings before the entrance to the more architecturally pleasing **Biniatrum** country house. Now our track skitters downhill to bring us onto the **Santa Galdana** road (Wp.21 48M) from where we have a simple stroll up to the ME-1 and back to our car. If you are finishing in **Ferreries** than continue on the dirt track opposite which cuts off the dogleg formed by the two roads.

A delightful route taking in the most impressive, but little known, quarry on Menorca and an abandoned army camp looking more like a deserted railway station but complete with ammunition storage caves (take a good torch). We link these surprises with a mixture of country tracks and trails along with three short sections of tarmac road. We discovered the quarry and camp during our road survey, but must give credit to Dodo Mackenzie who first pioneered this route.

Access by bus: There are buses from **Maó** and **Ciutadella** to **Alaior**. See appendices for details.

Access by car: take the **Son Bou** road from the **Alaior** bypass and after 1.4 kilometres, turn right onto an unsigned lane and park.

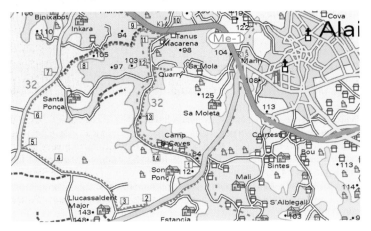

Most of our route is delightful country strolling so let's get the worst bit out of the way first - after this section it gets better all the time. From the entrance to the lane (Wp.1 0M) we cross over the road to walk up its left hand side for a steady ascent until a track goes off on our front right (Wp.2 13M). Walking up the cobbled track, we come up over 'sheep tunnels' onto a well-stabilised dirt track (Wp.3) to turn right. As the track gently rises we get views across the fields to **Alaior** town, the town's church tower and **Monte Toro**, providing a contrast to the bucolic landscape alongside our track. The fields beside the track give way to a belt of woodland, fields returning as we pass a well and *naveta*-style cattle shed (Wp.4) before coming to the **Sant Jaume** road (Wp.5 38M) opposite the entrance to **Son Sereni**.

Going right (N) we follow the wooded lane gently downhill past the entrance to **Lluc-quelber** (Wp.6) until we reach the old entrance to the impressive house of **Santa Ponça** (Wp.7 50M). Here the lane swings left while we continue straight ahead on a cobbled donkey trail down past the new entrance to **Santa Ponça**. Our well laid trail is reputed to date from roman times, its comparative steepness having saved it from tarmacking for vehicle use. As we come down the trail, we pass an interesting old quarry (Wp.8) on our left, our route levelling out to pass behind a large house before descending again and bringing the ME-1 road into view. Bushes push in on our trail (secateurs useful) as we come down the final slope before the trail runs out to reach the main road (Wp.9 67M).

Turning right (E) we walk alongside the ME-1 main road for 275 metres before leaving the fast traffic behind by turning right onto the country lane (Wp.10, 69M) serving **Villa Tanus**. This lane is little used apart from the houses and buildings near the ME-1 and after **Villa Torente** (Wp.11) bushes start to close down the road as our route runs into a hidden valley as we come to an anonymous junction (Wp.12 75M) where a track goes up to our left.

Most visitors to Menorca never even find this junction, let alone wonder what is up the track. Leaving the lane, we climb up the almost rock track to find a 'Santa Ponça' sign at the entrance to a quarry. Dwarfed by the vertical limestone walls we walk through the quarry's narrow entrance to be stunned by the vista unfolding in front of us.

Entering the quarry

The vertical walls run away to box in a large floor punctuated by a carved chapel and a marble slab proclaims 'La beleza es verdad, y la verdad es berleza' (beauty is truth, and truth is beauty). The scale of the quarry is just stunning. Along the high walls can be seen the lines of cutting out the limestone and carved stairs provided access to the different levels. Millions of tons of rock building slabs were carefully carved out of the mountain, providing the basis of many homes and the fortune that built the **Santa Ponça** country house.

When we've finished marvelling, we return to the country lane (Wp.12 0M) and continue strolling south past **Hort d'en Sands** as the flora pushes in on the narrow tarmac, while on our right limestone cliffs define the gorge. Crossing the watercourse (Wp.13 9M) our lane climbs up the remains of a sentry post and vehicle barrier followed by the first (Wp.14 17M) of three tunnels bored into the hillside; if you are considering exploring these ammunition storage caves come prepared with a good torch. Time hangs heavy on the little encampment, the style of buildings and the tunnels giving the air of a Victorian railway station that people have forgotten exists. After this second surprise we have an easy stroll along the lane back to our car.

Sited in a clifftop position overlooking the **Barranco de sa Cova** the Neolithic settlement of **Son Mercer** should be on everyone's 'must see' list, yet it is one of Menorca's least visited sites. Perhaps **Son Mercer** is undiscovered because there is a long dirt track to access the site, perhaps it is because the site has been missed by other writers; whatever the reason do see it now before the crowds arrive.

Technically, you can drive all the way to **Son Mercer** (if it's not wet) but you will miss out on the pastoral atmosphere as we stroll across unspoilt countryside to the Neolithic site.

Access by bus: Ferreries is served by routes from **Maó** and from **Ciutadella**. Details are in the appendices.

Access by car: Turn off the main road on the eastern side of **Ferreries** for on street parking. Alternatively take the **Es Migjorn Gran/Sant Tomás** road and turn off onto the **Son Mercer** access road (Wp.5) and park; reduce distance by 2.5 kilometres and time by 40 minutes.

Starting from **Ferreries** eastern roundabout (Wp.1 0M) we follow the **Es Migjorn Gran** road down alongside a massive concrete culvert that divides the new schools area from the old town. At a mini-roundabout (Wp.2 5M) we take the **Carrer Mallorca** street to walk up to its end at a T-junction where we go left to come onto the **Es Migjorn Gran** road (Wp.3 12M). Heading downhill (SE) we come down over a neat bridge (Wp.4) as the road runs between cultivated plots and forested hills for us to come to the **Son Mercer** access road on our right (Wp.5 23M).

'El Poblado Naveta de Son Merce' is signed up the concrete road as we set off (0M) up the steep ascent, the concrete reverting to dirt before we come to a break in the trees (Wp.6 6M); giving us the chance of a break to enjoy the views over the valley. It's a slogging ascent up through two hairpin bends until we come up past interesting megaliths (Wp.7 12M) to a junction marking the end of our vigorous ascent.

The pastoral scene of the **Son Mercer** plateau with its green fields and stone walls gently running down ahead of us is most welcome after that climb. **Estancia de Son Mercer** is an immaculate country house at the end of the main track while our route to 'Poblat Son Marcer de Baix' is signed down a gated road, remember to shut the gate, for an easy stroll down past a farm to another gate (Wp.8). Our route is simply to stay on the main track with the **Trebalúger** gorge developing on our right as we progress, passing a track dropping down to our left (Wp.9) and going through another gate (Wp.10) before coming up a small rise to the gate (Wp.11 33M) into the higgedly-piggledly **Son Mercer de Baix** farm.

Through the farm yard, the *poblat* is signed down the track which becomes a bramble tunnel as it crosses the valley floor and then climbs up to undulate along side of the deepening valley. Passing through gate posts (Wp.12) we have an easy stroll down to the next set of gateposts set in a stone wall (Wp.13 48M). It is all too easy to continue through the wall and find your way blocked a hundred metres further on by a locked steel gate and be left wondering how you could have missed the *poblat*. Before the gateposts we go left up the slope to go through a pair of wooden gates which reveal the 'El Poblado Naveta de Son Merce' signboard (Wp.14).

After the problems of finding the place, it is well worth exploring further. The *naveta* is particularly impressive with its roof stones supported on rock pillars.

Continuing up to the top of the Bronze Age settlement reveals more surprises as we find ourselves on the lip of the **Sa Cova** gorge above eighty metres of sheer limestone cliffs; do not go too near the edge. Here we have the best views of southern Menorca's limestone gorges, and just the ideal place to enjoy some refreshment before retracing our route back to **Ferreries**.

Menorca has many beautiful beaches and bays, and **Cala del Pilar** is up there with the best of them. This walk takes us to a beautiful, unspoilt castaway-style bay. Just remember to take swim wear and a picnic to make the most of it. Unfortunately, in recent times the cave houses have become hippified, which might detract from the attractiveness of this beautiful setting.

Somebody's guide book - we are not sure which - must describe this route as an easy stroll judging by the number of heavily burdened beach seekers in inadequate footwear that we see on these paths. Go prepared - the steep ascents and descents easily justify our 3 Walker rating.

Access by car: Turn north off the ME-1 onto the **Camí Son Felipe**. When the tarmac ends keep straight ahead on the dirt track (N) until you approach the trees then look to park on the grass near the trees and a wooden bike rack. If you reach a locked gate, you've gone too far.

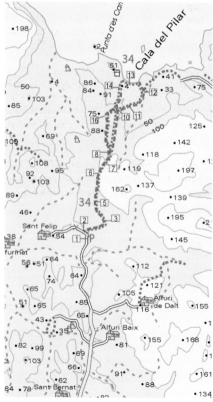

We park at the grassed area alongside the dirt road (Wp.1 0M) and stroll down the few metres to the walk's start at a gap in the stone wall (Wp.2). Keeping to the main track, we head up a sandy path through the holm oaks in a steady ascent (NE). Our gradient moderates as our route swings left (Wp.3 5M N), and then the path changes from hard dirt to soft sand for the next climb (Wp.4). The path levels out and reverts to hard dirt (Wp.5 9M) to overlook the valley on our left as we start to climb again (Wp.6 N) and then swings right (Wp.7 15M) to top a crest before starting to run downhill.

Pines have now replaced the oaks alongside the path as we come down to a fallen tree by a path to the left (Wp.8). We continue downhill in a gully until the water runoff goes down to our right (Wp.9), for us to continue on a smooth woodland path, walking beneath green boughs. Emerging from the trees, we come amongst sand dunes to continue downhill (N), and the sea comes into view.

We come down to the edge of the cliffs (Wp.10) where a walking trail climbs up from the beach, our preferred return route, before continuing down between dunes (Wp.11 27M) to an area of red mud on our left (Wp.12).

Cala del Pilar

Keeping to the left hand gully, we drop steadily down to the soft sand beach with its convenient bleached tree trunks ideal for sitting on (Wp.13 40M) - but watch out for the ants. Here you can relax on one of the least visited Menorcan coves, or stroll across the sand to the stone beach house.

After enjoying this five star bay, we return from the centre of the beach (Wp.14), following the clear track up to the base of the slope. Above us and on our left, a pair of substantial cave houses can be seen built in the top of the cliff as we struggle uphill through he soft sand. We come onto rock for an easier though still energetic climb up towards the cutting in the top of the cliffs.

Once on top of the cliffs (Wp.10), our outward route lies to our left but we go right, climbing up a dirt path to reach a crest (Wp.15). We keep to the main path as a small path goes right (Wp.16) to continue steadily up through the trees. Our path comes alongside a stone wall until the two diverge (Wp.17) and we climb gently up until we swing left to drop down to the fallen tree (Wp.8) of our outward route.

Now we retrace our steps through the wood and back to the car (80M). There is only one thing missing from this straightforward walk to an exciting destination - a *tipico*. As it's several kilometres to the nearest refreshment, don't forget to bring a picnic!

For historic content, this stroll is hard to beat, with relics from three different periods of Menorca's history. A search on the internet will reveal the current extent of interest in this region of Menorca, with digs taking place during the summer months. If you are interested in archaeology, then take a look inside the small museum housed in the same building as the snack bar, although the expensive and malodorous pay toilets next door are not recommended.

Considering the interest in the ancient history of this part of the island, it is surprising that this walking route has never appeared on a map until now.

Note: Although we have found no access problems on this route, please be aware that it crosses private land.

Access by car: on the ME-15 **Fornells** road, turn left at km 5, and then after four kilometres turn right on the **Camí de Cavalleria** and then it is another four kilometres north to the **Santa Teresa** museum and car park.

From the **Santa Teresa Museum** car park (Wp.1 0M), a trail leads quite steeply down (NNW) to cross the lane (SW) and continue down into a small valley, to join a dirt road (Wp.2 5M).

We go through a gate (W) to a junction of paths where we head (N) along the line of the valley. Our route curves left past the head of **Port de Sanitja**, for us to go through a wall (Wp.3) for a short climb (NNW) to another gap in a wall alongside the excavated remains of a Roman villa, the shapes and sizes of the individual rooms still clearly visible (Wp.4).

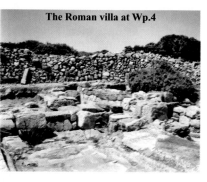

The Roman villa at Wp.4

On through the wall, and in the next field we find an unusually long, partly overgrown *naveta*. We climb a small rise and the **Torre de sa Nitja** comes into view, and we pass through another wall (Wp.5) for our stony path to head directly towards the old tower (Wp.6). We reach the tower in twenty minutes from the car park.

At the base of the tower

Unlike many of the coastal towers which can be viewed only from the outside, you can examine both the upper and lower floors of **Torre de sa Nitja**, though both are now used for shelter by the free-ranging sheep and goats!

We return by retracing our outward route. Basic refreshments are available from the little bar at the back of the **Santa Teresa** museum.

Although you can drive onto the **Cap de Cavalleria** peninsula on a good tarmac lane, walking this easy route to Menorca's northern point is much more enjoyable. We drive out on the **Camí de Cavalleria** as far as the museum at **Santa Teresa** and turn into its car park.

Roman remains at 5 minutes

You can buy simple refreshments from the museum's bar before setting off from beneath the shady trees on a path (N) which slopes gently down to the remains of a Roman village which straddles the tarmac lane (Wp.1 5M). From the village, we stroll along the tarmac lane with its views over the **Port de Sanitja** inlet to **Torre de sa Nitja** to a pair of wooden gates (Wp.2) - please close these after you.

It's easy strolling past dirt tracks which lead down to small bays on our left (W), until the lane swings left (NW) to start climbing onto the plateau at the end of the peninsula, though this hardly counts as an energetic climb.

When the lane swings back to the north by an old information point, we are back to easy strolling. A cliff-top ridge develops on our right as we walk towards the parking area (Wp.3 50M) before the light house, some fifty minutes from **Santa Teresa**. Walking past the parking area, we take paths west of the light house to come to old gun emplacements (Wp.4) at the top of the cliffs. We keep circling left to complete a circuit of the coastal battery and then follow a path (E) back to the parking area.

A tract-less mix of rock slabs and low scrub lies east of the lane, but crossing this is most rewarding. Aim for the low point in the cliff's ridge (Wp.5) and take care as you look over and down on the spectacular views of cliffs and churning sea.

We retrace our steps along the lane, mostly downhill this time, then up the path for celebratory drinks back beneath the shady trees.

Cala Pregonda is one of Menorca's most beautiful beaches, but public access has become restricted as landowners close off country roads. Our walking route offers the only open public access to this desirable destination. A picnic is recommended.

2 | 50 M | 4 km | 80m / 80m | and return | 3*

* at start and end

Access by car: Drive out of **Es Mercadal** on the **Camí de Tramuntana** minor road (N-NW) and turn right (E) before reaching **Pont de s'Alario**. Next go left (NE-N) onto the vast, wide dirt road to drive past the **Bar Binimel-Là**, leaving the car in the parking area behind the beach.

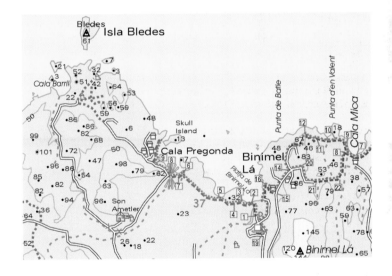

From the parking area (Wp.1 0M), we follow a path, passing the lagoon on our left to come onto the beach from where we head west (Wp.2 W). At the end of the beach (Wp.3), we take the inland path to come up to a crude gate (Wp.4). Stepping through the gate, we walk down and pass the next beach (Wp.5) and a dirt road which goes off to our left, as we climb a red earth slope inland of cliffs.

At the top of the climb we go through a wall, and **Cala Pregonda** comes into view - now, isn't that an idyllic location?

Our trail heads NW through green dunes, and **Cala Pregonda** comes back into view as we top a dune and then drop down towards the beach (Wp.6 17M).

Cala Pregonda

Past the beach, we climb up on red rock (Wp.7) and head for an electricity post, a steepish climb which brings us up to a gate onto the dirt road near the post (Wp.8 20M). We now have an easy stroll along the dirt road, accompanied by panoramic views over the bay and **Skull Island**.

The road drops down towards the bay where we take a path signed 'a la playa' (Wp.9) and drop down through the bushes onto this immaculate beach (25M). Take time to stroll along the beach and take advantage of this beautiful landscape while enjoying a swim and picnic.

We return by retracing our outward route. After the stiff climb up to the gate at the peak of the road, the return trip seems quite gentle!

Our search for the elusive, and largely non-existent **Camí de Cavalls**, opened our eyes to Menorca's coastal walking in regions we hadn't considered before. The result is a compact but adventurous route giving us a new way into the **Binimel-Là** beach, far better than driving down the wide 'corduroy' dirt road which is our car access to Walk 37; add the two routes together to enjoy some of the best northern beaches.

We have our preferred start, but given its limited parking, we offer an alternative start with masses of parking - plus this choice is more scenic, though you pay for this with a trudge across soft sand. For our approach to **Binimel-Là** from **Cala Mica**, we have our adventurous route above the cliffs combined with an easier but less spectacular return on an inland route.

Access by car: Follow the signs for **Cap de Cavalleria** from the ME-15 **Fornells** road. After turning onto the **Camí de Cavalleria** drive 2 kilometres to our preferred start point, or 3 kilometres to the **Cavalleria** car park for the alternative start.

Preferred Start

After parking alongside the road we start by going through the pedestrian entrance alongside the locked gate (Wp.1 0M) at the start of the **Platja de Ferragut** track. An easy stroll takes us down past a rock-barred track off to our right to a point where storm waters run off the track (Wp.2) to create a mud-sculpted landscape in the valley on our right.

Our preferred start point

As we continue, we come to views over the ocean (Wp.3), and passing wooden cycle racks, we come down to overlook the beach. Going uphill to our left, we come onto the start of a path (Wp.4 13M).

Alternative Start

From the sizeable roped-off parking area we walk over to the signboards to follow the track up to a pedestrian entrance through a wall (Wp.Alt1). Continuing on the track over a crest we come down to a turning circle to follow the path downhill to a *mirador* viewpoint (Wp.Alt2) for spectacular views down over the **Platjas de Cavalleria** and **Ferragut**; really one beach in geographical terms. Just past the *mirador*, we come to the top of a substantial wooden stairway (Wp.Alt3) which takes us down onto rocks at the eastern end of the beach.

Now we face 300 metres of soft-sand-slog to the life belt station at the centre of the beach, to then climb up the eroded gullies and slope to join our Preferred Start at the start of the path (Wp.4).

Continuation to Cala Mica

After an initial climb our narrow path runs along above steep slopes, almost cliffs, dropping down to the beach, to bring us to a stepped wall (Wp.5 16M). Over the wall our narrow trail pushes through the bush cutting across the headland at the end of the beach to cross a water-runoff. Now it is uphill to pass on the seaward side of 'decayed limestone teeth' and inland of a giant rock slab to views ahead to **Cala Mica**. Twisting along the top of the cliffs, our path, precarious at times amongst limestone boulders, then passes through a stone wall (Wp.6 23M) followed by a water-runoff.

Our path moves away from above the coastline to undulate along amongst the stunted bushes before coming above cliffs again and then running down to the seaward side of a house just inland of **Cala Mica** beach (Wp.7 29M). We continue on the faint path towards a breach in a stone wall. By the entrance to a gun position we climb up to cross the breach in the wall (Wp.8 31M) and a decision of which route to take for **Binimel-Là**.

Easy Route

If you like easy walking on well defined trails, or if you found the previous section vertiginous, then turn left (S) and follow our return route in reverse to **Binimel-Là**. If you up for some more adventure, read on.

Adventurous Route

Following the adventurous route

Turning right (N) we walk alongside the wall to find the start of a path (Wp.9 34M) just as the wall ends. Our path curves round over the headland (W) before climbing onto the next ridge (Wp.10) to drop steeply into the next valley on the seaward side of stunted bush; across from us traces and ways lead up the western side of the valley.

Across the floor of the valley we face a stiff climb up to a tumbled section of stone wall. Our way, formed more by water erosion than boot traffic, climbs up to become a path (Wp.11) gently ascending across folds in the land turns towards the sea to come almost to the edge of sheer cliffs (Wp.12 45M).

Now the only obvious route is to climb up the line of the cliffs just below the line of bushes to come to a rock section (Wp.13 51M) dividing clumps of bushes, to overlook **Binimel-Là** from our elevated position. A small, narrow,

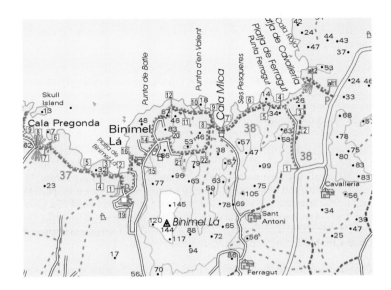

rock littered path starts twisting down towards an eroded track. Coming alongside we go over onto the track and now we can relax somewhat as we follow its route (S) over a 'Suzuki trap' and past an old track off to the right to arrive at a crossroads of tracks (Wp.14 59M); where our return, and easy route take the uphill track on the left.

Combined Finish

Turning right, we head down the main track to pass below **Can Roc** house and an old track to the right before coming to an unfinished house (Wp.15 64M). Ahead the main track rises to a crest while we take a narrow track, or wide trail, which drops down behind the house; stone stepping saving the route from the worst of water erosion. You could shortcut a loop of the track, but it's a much more relaxed style to stroll down to the corner (Wp.16) to swing south and come to the end of the beach and a well stabilised track (Wp.17). The beach is pretty, but more attractive to our eye is the **Bar Binimel-Là**, so we take the track round to the parking area to go through the beach entrance (Wp.18), where the bar's menu can give you food for thought as we climb up to take refreshments from its elevated position (Wp.19 76M).

Return to Cala Mica

Our Adventurous Route is safer and easier as an ascent than a descent, so follow this easy and quicker return to **Cala Mica**.

We return to the crossroads of tracks (Wp.14) and continue straight uphill to go through a cutting (Wp.20) into the next valley. Our track swings right (S) running downhill and then swings left (E), continuing downhill through another cutting (Wp.21). Erosion is gradually tearing the track apart, narrowing to a trail before we swing left (Wp.22) to follow the wall (N) back to its breach (Wp.8). From here we retrace our outward route to our chosen start point.

Beyond the white sand beach of **Son Parc** lies a deserted headland ending in spectacular cliffs, a complete contrast to the bustling **Fornells** peninsula on its west. Our route combines scenic views, bays and beaches before we climb up to the spectacularly sited 'House with no Name'. An easy walking route but do take plenty of water and sun protection as there is little shade en route.

3 | 3½ H | 12.5 km | 180m / 180m | and return | 3*

* at start and end

Access by bus: To **Son Parc** and then follow the 'Beach/Playa' signs. See appendices for bus details.

Access by car: After turning off the 'main' road continue past the golf course and at the start of the **Son Parc** development follow the 'Beach/Playa' signs down to the large car park (free) behind the beach.

> **Short Walk/Stroll**
>
> To **Cala Pudent** and return, 25 minutes each way.

Our start point on Son Parc beach

Starting from the bar/restaurant on the western end of **Son Parc** beach (Wp.1 0M) we cross the beach to go through a gap in the stone wall, following a stony path (N) which ascends gently alongside the azure waters of the bay towards a stone wall in the distance.

Through a gap in the wall, we pass through a second wall (Wp.2) before our stony path meanders uphill to a junction (Wp.3 14M).

Taking the right path, the sea comes back into view as we come to an old gun emplacement (Wp.4 15M), from where we enjoy excellent views back into the bay of **Son Parc**. Stepping a few metres left, we join the second path to follow its route (still stony) over a small rise, which brings the **House with No Name** into view in the distance at the end of the headland.

We drop down into a shallow valley and beach (Wp.5 20M) to follow a brown path (NW) that climbs gently before dropping down to overlook the cute bay of **Cala Pudent** (Wp.6). Our route swings left (26M) for us to walk gently up and away from **Cala Pudent** and then levels out to head WSW (Wp.7 30M) as our path widens to a track (W). Now pine trees accompany the *pistacia* and cistus bushes, taller here than on the exposed coast earlier on our route. The broad track(SSW) brings us to a T-junction with a main track (Wp.8 40M).

Now we swing right (N) to face the **House with No Name** at the head of the peninsula, exerting a brooding presence even at this distance. We have a choice of three tracks, all heading in the same general direction and coming together later on at a particularly large pine tree (Wp.9 49M).

Our easy stroll becomes slightly more difficult as the abandoned farm of **S'Albufereta** comes into view, our track becoming stony as it rises up the gentle slope. Old grey stone walls peep out of the bushes, lending a tired, abandoned air to the landscape as we approach the ruined house.

Passing the house entrance (Wp.10 55M), we walk up the stony track (N) to the edge of a valley where the main track swings right (Wp.11) as we go straight down a very stony minor track heading for the sea. Ahead, the continuation of our track is clearly visible as it climbs the slopes up to the old houses. It's a skittery descent alongside an old stone wall before we come alongside a tiny inlet with a white sand beach (Wp.12 67M) which looks across to the hustle and bustle of **Fornells** - what a contrast a few metres of sea makes!

Over a small ridge and past a second inlet with its own landing stage (Wp.13 72M), we now start to climb quite seriously. Sunglasses are recommended in sunny weather, to help reduce the reflected glare from the light stone surface as we toil up the relentless slopes. It is steadily upwards alongside a bush-filled valley on a straight ascent, before the road starts to zigzag (Wp.14 75M).

The gradient now eases for a comfortable walk past rosemary bushes, steadily ascending until, at the final zigzags (Wp.15 88M), we take a path to short-cut the road. Passing a cave and stone quarry on our right, we cross the road onto another path (N) before rejoining the road for the last bend up to the first house (Wp.16). This is not an old farm, but a military officers' house, and we turn left to cross the open ground and pass the barracks building to come up onto the gun positions (Wp.17 98M) above the cliffs at the head of the peninsula.

At 122 metres altitude, the **Mola de Fornells** is easily the highest point in this region, an old civil war look-out point giving spectacular cliff views from our elevated position. Having climbed up to this splendidly isolated cliff top position it would be a waste to simply turn straight round to return, so bring provisions so you can take your time enjoying the views. Take care when exploring on the **Mola de Fornells**, as none of the houses or gun pits are maintained, and the cliffs are sheer.

When we are satiated with the isolation and the views, we return by our outward route to sample the refreshments on the bar terrace overlooking **Son Parc** beach before our final departure.

40 JOHN'S ROUTE: NA MACARET CIRCULAR

It's very unusual for us to be guided round a walking route. 99% of the time we are providing the guidance information, but this time John Devine (see appendices) suggested he showed us a northern route; so here is John's Route. The walking is easy, more of an extended stroll rather than a challenge, through comfortable countryside.

Access by car: From the ME-9/ME-7 roundabout, continue north on the ME-9 and follow the road signs for **Na Macaret**. Coming into the urbanisation, go left at the first roundabout and right at the second to come to a parking square by our start point.

Our start point is at the bar (Wp.1 0M) to walk up past the boat house cottages and across a roundabout, continuing on to the end of the street at **Casa de los Vientos** where we take the faint trail that leaves the turning circle (Wp.2 5M) to head across the stony plateau (W) towards **Arenal d'en Castell**. A cairn marks the edge of the cliffs, more cairns confirming the faint trail as we swing towards **Punta Grossa** (N) before moving away from the cliff edge to head west again towards a large sea-cave.

The faint trail meanders between little limestone knife-edges as we come to a junction (Wp.3 16M); ahead, the main trail goes towards **Arenal** resort, while we keep right on a fainter trail which curves around a rocky inlet and across a shallow valley to come up onto a street between two bungalows (Wp.4 21M).

At the top of the street we turn left and then keep right at a traffic island, as we pass the rather bland bungalows of **Punta Grossa** to turn down **Carrer des Verderol** (Wp.5 28M). We stroll down between the bungalows, and as the street swings right (Wp.6) we drop down oversize steps to come amongst pines. A dirt track extension of a street guides us out onto the end of **Arenal** beach. Now we have a legionnaire style soft-sand slog over to the steps by the café (Wp.7 39M), which take us up to the service road and on up to the main street, and uphill again through the tourist sprawl until we come to a dirt track (Wp.8 43M) where we can escape into the countryside.

Now we head out (W) across the heathland plateau in a gentle ascent, the track reducing to trail before splitting, then coming together again before we pass through a break in a stone wall (Wp.9 52M). The main trail continues straight ahead while we turn left, following the line of the wall on a track/trail to pass the end of a **Son Parc** street and come onto a dirt track (Wp.10 55M).

Going left, we stroll gently downhill, passing a logging track on our left before coming to a section where the track is being prepared for tarmacking (Wp.11 October 2004 part of the expansion at **Son Parc**), then arriving at a T-junction (Wp.12 62M) with a metalled road signed as a cul-de-sac. Going left

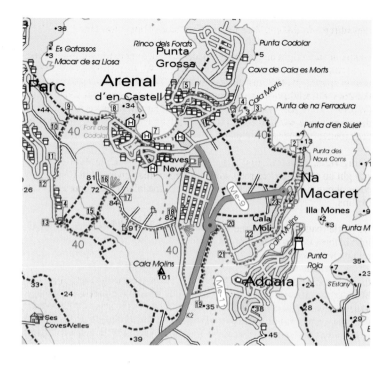

(S) we stroll down to the end of the tarmac and the last villa, N°245 **Casa Sulemanyah** (Wp.13 66M), to take a dirt track which goes left beside a stone wall. Ignoring the first made gap in the wall, we continue to the second gap (Wp.14) where go right to come in amongst the pine woods.

A broad trail leads us through the trees, passing first a track to the left and then one to the right as we start heading uphill to a crossroads of tracks (Wp.15) where we continue uphill, the track getting rougher as we climb. Passing a fenced hut, we come to a broad dirt road (Wp16 85M) which looks ripe for evolving into a new urbanisation before too long. Turning right, it's still uphill until we reach the crest at another broad dirt road (Wp.17) running down towards **Arenal**. Now we have an easy stroll, the wide dirt road keeping to the spine to pass another crossroads and then another; this one with an historic JCB.

The broad trail through the pines

After passing three more dirt tracks to the right we reach a tarmac road (Wp.18 96M) with the 'Coves Noves II' development sign; judging by the size of these dirt roads, this could become an extension of bungalow land.

Before heading right on the tarmac road, we walk over to the wind-bent pines for views down over **Addaia** and **Na Macaret**. We then stroll down the road past an apartment block to the Me-9 junction. Taking care, we cross over onto the **Port d'Addaia** road, and in twenty metres go left onto a woodland path (Wp.19 110M). Keeping left at a junction, we have a pleasant stroll through the pines before our trail comes up to parallel the ME-9 to bring us onto the back road to **Na Macaret** (Wp.20 119M).

Going right, we stroll down the pavement towards **Cala Molí**, keeping straight on a once-barred road when the 'main' road swings left (Wp.21), to come above the bamboo thickets which choke the inland watercourse of **Cala Molins**.

Cala Molins

Our little road runs above the inlet before curving back up to rejoin the 'main' road (Wp.22 132M) where we go right through the houses of **Cala Molí** until, coming into **Na Macaret**, we take a pedestrian walkway on our right (Wp.23) to go down the stepped decent into the square (142M) of our start point ready for refreshments in **Bar Macaret**.

GPS Waypoints for the walking routes included in Walk! Menorca are quoted in Latitude/Longitude for the WGS84 Datum; the default datum for GPS receivers. Before loading waypoints into your GPS unit please read 'Using GPS on Menorca' on page 19. To input the waypoints into your GPS set the 'location format' to 'hddd° .mm.mmm' and check that your datum is set to WGS84.

Full GPS Track and Waypoint files for these 38 walking routes, in Oziexplorer format files, are available on our PNFs (Personal Navigator Files) CD available for £7.99 from Discovery Walking Guides Ltd. See our websites for more information:-

www.walking.demon.co.uk and **www.dwgwalking.co.uk**

3. FROM TOWN TO TOWN - MAÓ TO ES CASTELL

Wp	N	E
1	39 53.109	4 16.783
2	39 53.090	4 16.830
3	39 52.984	4 17.005
4	39 52.987	4 17.063

4. CALA FIGUERA - TREPUCÓ - SANT LLUÍS

Wp	N	E
1	39 52.988	4 16.475
2	39 52.573	4 16.155
3	39 52.505	4 16.046
4	39 52.507	4 16.015
5	39 52.447	4 15.964
6	39 52.433	4 15.979
7	39 52.253	4 15.898
8	39 51.882	4 15.910
9	39 51.633	4 16.122
10	39 51.457	4 15.996
11	39 51.166	4 15.569

5. SANT LLUÍS - POU NOU - TREBALÚGER

Wp	N	E
1	39 50.973	4 15.603
2	39 50.957	4 15.778
3	39 50.816	4 15.857
4	39 50.866	4 15.879
5	39 50.888	4 16.021
6	39 50.939	4 16.129
7	39 50.812	4 16.465
8	39 50.956	4 16.531
9	39 51.188	4 16.535
10	39 51.299	4 16.580
11	39 51.344	4 16.571
12	39 51.352	4 16.480

6. GUARDS, GUARDS!

Wp	N	E
1	39 51.877	4 18.004
2	39 51.877	4 17.953
3	39 51.842	4 17.908
4	39 51.772	4 17.963
5	39 51.835	4 18.120
6	39 51.782	4 18.241
7	39 51.741	4 18.279
8	39 51.655	4 18.287
9	39 51.578	4 18.244
10	39 51.561	4 18.235
11	39 51.680	4 18.177
12	39 51.687	4 18.133
13	39 51.706	4 18.026

7. BINISSAIDA - TORRE D'EN PUNYAT CIRCULAR

Wp	N	E
1	39 51.200	4 17.771
2	39 51.416	4 17.663
3	39 51.454	4 18.086
4	39 51.571	4 18.073
5	39 51.609	4 18.207
6	39 51.562	4 18.242
7	39 51.560	4 18.303
8	39 51.439	4 18.338
9	39 51.324	4 18.317
10	39 51.193	4 18.316
11	39 50.956	4 18.418
12	39 50.948	4 18.337
13	39 51.007	4 18.323
14	39 51.019	4 18.282
15	39 51.027	4 18.193
16	39 51.021	4 18.061
17	39 51.047	4 17.993
18	39 51.194	4 17.870
19	39 51.235	4 17.865

8. LINKING THE RESORTS: BINIBÉQUER VELL - PUNTA PRIMA

Wp	N	E
1	39 49.360	4 13.828
2	39 49.108	4 14.182
3	39 49.058	4 14.347
4	39 49.059	4 14.479
5	39 49.012	4 14.560
6	39 48.968	4 14.707
7	39 49.013	4 14.743
8	39 49.007	4 14.777
9	39 48.956	4 14.888
10	39 48.860	4 15.179
11	39 48.791	4 15.364
12	39 48.764	4 15.482
13	39 48.742	4 15.702
14	39 48.743	4 15.743
15	39 48.773	4 15.815
16	39 48.673	4 15.823
17	39 48.619	4 15.988
18	39 48.623	4 16.606
19	39 48.685	4 16.766
20	39 48.718	4 16.855
21	39 48.844	4 16.816

9. COASTAL DISCOVERY

Wp	N	E
1	39 48.898	4 16.947
2	39 48.983	4 17.215
3	39 49.079	4 17.366
4	39 49.365	4 17.693
5	39 49.525	4 17.626
6	39 49.688	4 17.651
7	39 49.734	4 17.507
8	39 49.766	4 17.828
9	39 49.933	4 17.941

10.
FROM NEW TO OLD:
S'ALGAR - BINISSAIDA +
CALA D'ES RAFALET

Wp	N	E
1	39 50.029	4 17.776
2	39 50.083	4 17.591
3	39 50.249	4 17.645
4	39 50.347	4 17.640
5	39 50.498	4 17.644
6	39 50.473	4 17.851
7	39 50.525	4 17.703
8	39 50.614	4 17.757
9	39 50.716	4 17.710
10	39 50.893	4 17.444
11	39 50.962	4 17.589
12	39 51.195	4 17.840
13	39 51.313	4 17.713
14	39 51.418	4 17.664
15	39 51.460	4 18.086
16	39 51.705	4 18.030
17	39 51.764	4 17.973
18	39 51.843	4 17.917
19	39 51.880	4 17.955
20	39 52.144	4 17.876
21	39 52.249	4 17.730
22	39 52.647	4 17.388

11.
CAMÍ DE BINIATAP

Wp	N	E
1	39 51.200	4 17.771
2	39 51.416	4 17.663
3	39 51.646	4 17.519
4	39 51.718	4 17.211
5	39 51.760	4 17.120
6	39 51.973	4 17.005
7	39 52.496	4 16.744
8	39 52.878	4 16.628
9	39 52.960	4 16.519
10	39 52.985	4 16.477

12.
AN HISTORICAL TOUR

Wp	N	E
1	39 52.960	4 14.194
2	39 52.938	4 14.075
3	39 52.882	4 13.877
4	39 52.880	4 13.705
5	39 52.732	4 13.459
6	39 52.664	4 13.330
7	39 52.754	4 13.211
8	39 52.840	4 13.247
9	39 53.027	4 13.321
10	39 53.003	4 13.382
11	39 53.369	4 13.609
12	39 53.421	4 13.793
13	39 53.279	4 14.431
14	39 53.107	4 14.284

13.
MORE HISTORICAL SIGHTS:
MAÓ - TALATÍ DE DALT -
RAFAL RUBÍ VELL

Wp	N	E
1	39 53.279	4 14.431
2	39 53.306	4 14.099
3	39 53.426	4 13.796
4	39 53.371	4 13.613
5	39 53.625	4 13.055
6	39 53.644	4 12.935
7	39 53.628	4 12.022
8	39 54.158	4 11.664
9	39 54.315	4 11.434
10	39 54.479	4 11.457
11	39 54.443	4 11.383

14.
S'ALBUFERA: THE THREE ROUTES

Wp	N	E
B1	39 56.949	4 16.042
B2	39 57.167	4 15.860
B3	39 57.140	4 15.802
B4	39 57.082	4 15.781
B5	39 57.038	4 15.782
B6	39 56.861	4 15.838
B7	39 56.788	4 15.871
B8	39 56.775	4 15.913
B9	39 56.762	4 15.970
RG1	39 56.612	4 15.094
R2	39 56.632	4 15.183
R3	39 56.655	4 15.189
R4	39 56.701	4 15.308
R5	39 56.692	4 15.359
R6	39 56.687	4 15.392
R7	39 56.771	4 15.565
G2	39 56.683	4 14.988
G3	39 56.778	4 14.846
G4	39 56.739	4 14.857
G5	39 56.696	4 14.892

15.
ES GRAU PENINSULA

Wp	N	E
1	39 56.949	4 16.042
2	39 57.167	4 15.860
3	39 57.218	4 15.941
4	39 57.243	4 15.914
5	39 57.280	4 15.910
6	39 57.299	4 15.844
7	39 57.309	4 15.778
8	39 57.336	4 15.812
9	39 57.355	4 15.879
10	39 57.377	4 15.994
11	39 57.303	4 16.070
12	39 57.313	4 16.091
13	39 57.338	4 16.139
14	39 57.415	4 16.142
15	39 57.566	4 16.062
16	39 57.531	4 15.972
17	39 57.469	4 15.923
18	39 57.478	4 15.858
19	39 57.470	4 15.833

16.
TORRE BLANCA

Wp	N	E
1	39 56.949	4 16.042
2	39 57.167	4 15.860
3	39 57.218	4 15.941
4	39 57.243	4 15.914
5	39 57.280	4 15.910
6	39 57.299	4 15.844
7	39 57.309	4 15.778
8	39 57.470	4 15.833
9	39 57.524	4 15.750
10	39 57.550	4 15.725
11	39 57.691	4 15.738
12	39 57.731	4 15.605
13	39 57.791	4 15.415
14	39 57.748	4 15.307
15	39 57.795	4 15.200
16	39 57.805	4 14.878
17	39 57.832	4 14.798
18	39 57.950	4 14.666
19	39 57.980	4 14.548
20	39 57.800	4 14.627
21	39 57.632	4 14.699
22	39 57.563	4 14.740
23	39 57.527	4 14.725
24	39 57.367	4 15.004
25	39 57.279	4 15.091
26	39 57.218	4 15.244
27	39 57.301	4 15.360
28	39 57.354	4 15.412
29	39 57.434	4 15.556

17.
CAP DE FAVARITX

Wp	N	E
1	39 59.805	4 15.409
2	39 59.635	4 15.253
3	39 59.603	4 15.178
4	39 59.549	4 15.265
5	39 59.431	4 15.260
6	39 59.371	4 15.289
7	39 59.276	4 15.331
8	39 59.264	4 15.349
9	39 59.216	4 15.428
10	39 59.198	4 15.552

18.
CALA MESQUIDA - ES GRAU

Wp	N	E
1	39 54.964	4 17.159
2	39 55.050	4 17.180
3	39 55.054	4 17.116
4	39 55.201	4 17.108
5	39 55.331	4 17.041
6	39 55.421	4 17.032
7	39 55.526	4 16.925
8	39 55.799	4 16.658
9	39 55.779	4 16.529
10	39 55.814	4 16.515
11	39 55.897	4 16.556
12	39 55.982	4 16.454
13	39 56.053	4 16.368
14	39 56.452	4 16.629
15	39 56.687	4 16.741
16	39 56.719	4 16.674
17	39 56.933	4 16.635
18	39 56.948	4 16.496
19	39 56.959	4 16.416
20	39 56.989	4 16.237
21	39 56.993	4 16.107

19.
CALA BLANCA TO CAP D'ARTRUTX

Wp	N	E
1	39 57.889	3 49.988
2	39 57.740	3 50.077
3	39 57.460	3 49.949
4	39 57.310	3 49.835
5	39 57.116	3 49.501
6	39 56.627	3 49.568
7	39 56.380	3 49.625
8	39 56.361	3 49.535
9	39 56.102	3 49.379
10	39 55.901	3 49.393
11	39 55.577	3 49.290
12	39 55.412	3 49.441
13	39 55.613	3 49.564

20.
GALDANA GORGE

Wp	N	E
1	39 56.414	3 57.569
2	39 56.642	3 57.737
3	39 56.688	3 57.687
4	39 56.728	3 57.625
5	39 56.850	3 57.787
6	39 56.914	3 57.835
7	39 56.988	3 57.749
8	39 57.121	3 57.756
9	39 57.425	3 57.781
10	39 57.559	3 57.796
11	39 57.595	3 57.715
12	39 57.667	3 57.852

21.
CALA GALDANA TO CALA MACARELLA

Wp	N	E
1	39 56.331	3 57.425
2	39 56.279	3 57.260
3	39 56.255	3 57.085
4	39 56.278	3 56.447
5	39 56.300	3 56.396
6	39 56.308	3 56.272

22.
CALA MACARELLA TO CIUTADELLA

Wp	N	E
1	39 56.310	3 56.273
2	39 56.529	3 56.152
3	39 56.616	3 56.232
4	39 56.902	3 56.539
5	39 57.486	3 56.171
6	39 57.566	3 56.098
7	39 57.768	3 55.904
8	39 58.162	3 54.913
9	39 58.471	3 54.331
10	39 58.432	3 54.079
11	39 58.120	3 52.905
12	39 58.522	3 52.495
13	39 58.720	3 52.045
14	39 59.611	3 50.923
15	39 59.783	3 50.732

23.
CALA GALDANA - CALA MITJANA - CALA TREBALÚGER + A WOODLAND STROLL

Wp	N	E
1	39 56.381	3 57.971
2	39 56.184	3 57.815
3	39 56.096	3 57.985
4	39 56.077	3 58.092
5	39 55.988	3 58.111
6	39 56.093	3 58.386
7	39 56.077	3 58.410
8	39 56.065	3 58.392
9	39 56.029	3 58.411
10	39 56.018	3 58.429
11	39 56.000	3 58.549
12	39 55.978	3 58.649
13	39 55.966	3 58.780
14	39 55.958	3 58.868
15	39 55.927	3 59.040
16	39 55.909	3 59.132
17	39 55.846	3 59.258
18	39 55.858	3 59.285
19	39 56.187	3 58.452
20	39 56.303	3 58.603
21	39 56.381	3 58.643
22	39 56.537	3 58.655
23	39 56.620	3 58.984

24.
CALA GALDANA TO CALA'N BOSCH

Wp	N	E
1	39 56.331	3 57.425
2	39 56.279	3 57.260
3	39 56.255	3 57.085
4	39 56.278	3 56.447
5	39 56.300	3 56.396
6	39 56.308	3 56.272
7	39 56.318	3 56.105
8	39 56.319	3 56.062
9	39 56.293	3 56.003
10	39 56.267	3 56.015
11	39 56.207	3 56.125
12	39 56.307	3 55.971
13	39 56.191	3 55.710
14	39 56.167	3 55.650
15	39 56.064	3 55.389
16	39 55.994	3 54.893
17	39 55.964	3 54.879
18	39 55.922	3 54.823
19	39 55.922	3 54.790
20	39 55.809	3 54.700
21	39 55.759	3 54.722
22	39 55.589	3 54.580
23	39 55.624	3 54.242
24	39 55.607	3 54.103
25	39 55.585	3 54.080
26	39 55.686	3 53.728
27	39 55.672	3 53.471
28	39 55.629	3 53.447
29	39 55.537	3 53.390
30	39 55.439	3 53.229
31	39 55.446	3 53.052
32	39 55.395	3 52.994
33	39 55.357	3 52.501
34	39 55.375	3 52.397
35	39 55.492	3 52.132
36	39 55.461	3 51.911
37	39 55.360	3 51.921
38	39 55.355	3 51.655
39	39 55.407	3 51.337
40	39 55.525	3 50.710
41	39 55.638	3 50.204

25.
FORTS ANCIENT AND MODERN: TORRE D'EN GALMÉS - LLUC AL LARI

Wp	N	E
1	39 54.182	4 06.944
2	39 54.382	4 06.950
3	39 54.247	4 06.725

Wp	N	E
4	39 53.953	4 06.415
5	39 53.547	4 05.831
6	39 53.452	4 05.685
7	39 53.417	4 05.429
8	39 53.272	4 05.279
9	39 53.235	4 05.232
10	39 53.389	4 05.609

26.

SANT TOMÁS TO SON BOU

Wp	N	E
1	39 54.763	4 02.620
2	39 54.695	4 02.677
3	39 54.632	4 02.689
4	39 54.465	4 03.182
5	39 54.460	4 03.310
6	39 54.078	4 04.136
7	39 53.992	4 04.262
8	39 53.771	4 04.712

27.

SANT TOMÁS TO COVA D'ES COLOMS

Wp	N	E
1	39 55.031	4 01.994
2	39 55.121	4 01.773
3	39 55.213	4 01.586
4	39 55.288	4 01.496
5	39 55.420	4 01.501
6	39 55.484	4 01.671
7	39 55.702	4 01.764
8	39 55.809	4 01.961
9	39 55.814	4 02.204
10	39 55.904	4 02.269
11	39 55.988	4 02.296
12	39 55.970	4 02.326
13	39 56.047	4 02.302
14	39 56.135	4 02.266
15	39 56.033	4 02.041
16	39 55.908	4 01.838
17	39 55.528	4 01.450
18	39 56.255	4 02.410
19	39 56.393	4 02.566
20	39 56.588	4 02.734
21	39 56.702	4 02.801

28.

ES MIGJORN GRAN TO SANT TOMÁS

Wp	N	E
1	39 56.702	4 02.801
2	39 56.588	4 02.734
3	39 56.329	4 03.050
4	39 56.187	4 03.091
5	39 56.071	4 03.130
6	39 56.086	4 03.181
7	39 56.014	4 03.143
8	39 55.593	4 02.987
W1	39 55.538	4 02.882
W2	39 55.426	4 02.745
W3	39 55.239	4 02.648
W4	39 55.198	4 02.408
W5	39 55.095	4 02.281
W6	39 55.010	4 02.185
E1	39 55.163	4 03.046
E2	39 55.080	4 03.095
E3	39 54.990	4 02.986

29.

CALAS COVES CIRCULAR

Wp	N	E
1	39 52.720	4 09.862
2	39 52.172	4 09.017
3	39 51.905	4 08.825
4	39 51.862	4 08.787
5	39 51.893	4 08.701
6	39 51.953	4 08.629
7	39 52.033	4 08.639
8	39 52.160	4 08.428
9	39 52.006	4 08.449
10	39 51.950	4 08.437
11	39 51.849	4 08.473
12	39 51.826	4 08.590
B1	39 51.891	4 08.222
B2	39 51.856	4 08.319
B3	39 51.820	4 08.389
B4	39 51.821	4 08.423

30.

SANTA AGUEDA

Wp	N	E
1	40 01.200	4 00.082
2	40 01.325	4 00.216
3	40 01.360	4 00.275
4	40 01.414	4 00.382
5	40 01.421	4 00.408
6	40 01.445	4 00.380
7	40 01.562	4 00.414
8	40 01.630	4 00.397
9	40 01.616	4 00.418
10	40 01.645	4 00.399
11	40 01.635	4 00.472

31.

FERRERIES TO GALDANA GORGE

Wp	N	E
1	39 59.054	4 00.414
2	39 59.182	4 00.262
3	39 59.228	3 59.465
4	39 59.333	3 59.156
5	39 59.299	3 59.083
6	39 59.205	3 58.988
7	39 58.894	3 58.861
8	39 58.613	3 58.648
9	39 58.860	3 58.451
10	39 58.834	3 58.414
11	39 58.702	3 58.260
12	39 58.684	3 58.377
13	39 58.580	3 58.045
14	39 58.577	3 57.943
15	39 58.553	3 58.786
16	39 58.636	3 58.990
17	39 58.741	3 59.498
18	39 58.745	3 59.692
19	39 58.727	3 59.833
20	39 58.759	3 59.940
21	39 58.961	4 00.265

32.

ALAIOR CIRCULAR

Wp	N	E
1	39 55.415	4 07.633
2	39 55.194	4 07.201
3	39 55.162	4 06.962
4	39 55.423	4 06.442
5	39 55.534	4 06.225
6	39 55.735	4 06.253
7	39 55.930	4 06.505
8	39 56.052	4 06.672
9	39 56.230	4 07.207
10	39 56.201	4 07.396
11	39 56.146	4 07.288
12	39 56.017	4 07.250
13	39 55.705	4 07.142
14	39 55.525	4 07.284

33.

FERRERIES TO SON MERCER

Wp	N	E
1	39 59.118	4 00.989
2	39 58.972	4 00.824
3	39 58.768	4 00.805
4	39 58.681	4 00.947
5	39 58.634	4 01.268
6	39 58.575	4 01.054
7	39 58.448	4 01.023
8	39 58.289	4 01.047
9	39 58.245	4 01.005
10	39 57.998	4 00.704
11	39 57.827	4 00.560
12	39 57.496	4 00.563
13	39 57.296	4 00.311
14	39 57.283	4 00.343
15	39 57.275	4 00.423

34.

CALA PILAR

Wp	N	E
1	40 02.163	3 58.374
2	40 02.191	3 58.376
3	40 02.276	3 58.495
4	40 02.324	3 58.464
5	40 02.386	3 58.448
6	40 02.535	3 58.453
7	40 02.603	3 58.510

Wp	N	E
8	40 02.667	3 58.519
9	40 02.740	3 58.546
10	40 02.922	3 58.588
11	40 02.952	3 58.670
12	40 03.008	3 58.765
13	40 03.052	3 58.681
14	40 03.027	3 58.626
15	40 02.896	3 58.534
16	40 02.879	3 58.510
17	40 02.743	3 58.501

35.
TORRE DE SA NITJA - HISTORIC SURPRISES

Wp	N	E
1	40 03.948	4 05.312
2	40 04.001	4 05.288
3	40 04.091	4 05.249
4	40 04.154	4 05.236
5	40 04.222	4 05.169
6	40 04.403	4 05.040

36.
CAP DE CAVALLERIA

Wp	N	E
1	40 04.045	4 05.379
2	40 04.167	4 05.417
3	40 05.298	4 05.531
4	40 05.323	4 05.438
5	40 05.229	4 05.586

37.
CALA PREGONDA

Wp	N	E
1	40 03.011	4 03.202
2	40 03.103	4 03.195
3	40 03.101	4 03.121
4	40 03.078	4 03.033
5	40 03.124	4 02.941
6	40 03.272	4 02.641
7	40 03.253	4 02.599
8	40 03.283	4 02.551
9	40 03.343	4 02.423

38.
CAP DE CAVALLERIA TO BINIMEL-LÁ

Wp	N	E
1	40 03.166	4 04.561
2	40 03.362	4 04.552
3	40 03.437	4 04.531
4	40 03.494	4 04.460
5	40 03.498	4 04.376
6	40 03.457	4 04.162
7	40 03.357	4 03.950
8	40 03.389	4 03.896
9	40 03.434	4 03.892
10	40 03.454	4 03.804
11	40 03.471	4 03.691
12	40 03.503	4 03.617
13	40 03.448	4 03.547
14	40 03.308	4 03.491
15	40 03.181	4 03.376
16	40 03.211	4 03.296
17	40 03.137	4 03.278
18	40 03.002	4 03.224
19	40 02.947	4 03.268
20	40 03.316	4 03.558
21	40 03.251	4 03.853
Alt1	40 03.581	4 04.778
Alt2	40 03.646	4 04.646
Alt3	40 03.664	4 04.624

39.
PLAYA DE SON PARC TO THE HOUSE WITH NO NAME

Wp	N	E
1	40 01.973	4 09.602
2	40 02.201	4 09.607
3	40 02.286	4 09.656
4	40 02.327	4 09.691
5	40 02.471	4 09.590
6	40 02.591	4 09.530
7	40 02.516	4 09.346
8	40 02.279	4 08.954
9	40 02.629	4 08.857
10	40 02.909	4 08.816
11	40 03.101	4 08.765
12	40 03.324	4 08.623
13	40 03.425	4 08.493
14	40 03.567	4 08.484
15	40 03.802	4 08.538
16	40 03.875	4 08.534
17	40 03.972	4 08.554

40.
JOHN'S ROUTE: NA MACARET CIRCULAR

Wp	N	E
1	40 01.000	4 12.038
2	40 01.206	4 12.076
3	40 01.422	4 11.687
4	40 01.459	4 11.560
5	40 01.538	4 11.224
6	40 01.495	4 11.233
7	40 01.297	4 10.879
8	40 01.417	4 10.657
9	40 01.438	4 10.315
10	40 01.310	4 10.217
11	40 01.154	4 10.212
12	40 01.073	4 10.178
13	40 00.835	4 10.213
14	40 00.841	4 10.273
15	40 00.852	4 10.520
16	40 01.016	4 10.604
17	40 00.968	4 10.688
18	40 00.844	4 11.125
19	40 00.407	4 11.261
20	40 00.802	4 11.401
21	40 00.653	4 11.584
22	40 00.708	4 11.681
23	40 00.988	4 11.983

GLOSSARY

This glossary contains Spanish words found in the text (shown in *italics*),
plus other local words that you may encounter.

SPANISH	CATALÁN	
a		
agua, con/sin gas		water, fizzy/still
aljibe	**aljub**	ancient cistern/reservoir
alto	**dalt**	high, upper
área recreativa		picnic spot, usually with barbecues, toilets, water
atalaia	**atalaya**	ancient watch-tower
avenida	**avinguda**	avenue
ayuntamiento	**ayuntament**	town hall
b		
bajo	**baix**	low
bajo	**avall**	lower
barranco	**barranc**	gorge, ravine
basilica		early Christian Romanesque church
	bastió	stronghold
botadores		stone steps in country walls
c		
cala		creek, small bay, sometimes just a tiny coastal indentation
cala		inlet, cove
calle	**carrer**	street
	caló	little cove
camino	**camí**	road, path or way
camino real	**camí reial**	royal road, once a major donkey trail
campo		countryside, field
canaleta	**siquia**	man-made water channel, including anything from a concrete canal to delicately arched aqueducts
calle	**carrer**	street
carritx	**carritx**	pampas-like grass
casa	**can/ca**	house of (as *chez* in French)
caseta		hut, cabin, small house
castillo	**castell**	castle
cingles		cliffs, crags; most often used to describe the sort of short, abrupt cliffs that typically define the rounded summits of many Catalán and Mallorcan mountains
ciudad	**ciutat**	city
coll		saddle, neck or pass
correos		post office
costa		coast
e		
embalse		reservoir
ermita		hermitage, small church, shrine
f		
faro	**far**	lighthouse
fiesta		festival, public holiday
finca	**lluc**	farm
forn de calc	**horno de calç**	lime kiln
fuente	**font**	spring, well
h		
hostal		hostel, lodgings

hypostyle		prehistoric chamber, partly underground, with stone roof supported on pillars

I

iglesia	*església*	church

l

lavadero		public laundry area
llano	*pla*	plain, flat land

j

	jutjat	lawcourts

m

medio	*mig*	middle
mercado	*mercat*	market
mirador		viewing point, sometimes with man-made facilities, more often a natural place with a good view
morro		snout or muzzle, a rounded summit
muelle	*moll*	harbour, quay
museo	*museo*	museum

n

	naveta	prehistoric boat-shaped building
nuevo	*nou*	new

p

palacio	*palau*	palace
parada		bus stop
particular		private
paseo	*passeig*	walkway
peatones		pedestrians
peña	*penya/penyal*	rock or boulder, used for a knoll or pinnacle on a ridge
pico	*puig*	translates as 'hill' or 'height', though more often a peak or mountain
pista		dirt road
pista forestal		forest road
pistacia lentiscus		the shrub/tree threatening to inhabit the entire island
playa	*platja*	beach
plaza	*plaça*	town square
pozo	*pou*	well
privado		private
prohibido el paso		no entry
puerto	*port*	port, mountain pass

r

refugio		mountain refuge, some offering basic overnight accommodation

s

santo/a	*san/sant*	saint
santuario	*santuari*	monastery, hermitage
sendero	*senda*	footpath, trail
sitja (pl. sitjes)	*sitja*	charcoal burning area or circle
su	*son, sa, ses*	his, her, their

t

	talaiot	prehistoric cone-shaped mound
	taula	prehistoruc T-shaped stone monument
tipico		typical, locals' café/bar
toro bravo		wild bull
torre		tower, often a coastal watchtower built to warn of approaching pirates, or a Moorish lookout tower
torrente	*torrent*	stream

u

urbanización		housing development

Please note:
Telephone numbers are shown in red, and fax numbers in blue, and we show the entire number you need to dial from outside Spain. From within Spain, omit the 00 34.

MAPS & BOOKS

Two Spanish organisations publish the closest equivalents to traditional Ordnance Survey style maps. However, bear in mind that their publications are only occasionally updated. We have not found them available on the island.

Centro Nacional de Información Geográfica
Oficina Central, Monte Esquinza, 41
28010 Madrid, Spain
00 34 91 5979453   00 34 91 5532913
www.cnig.es   consulta@cnig.es.

Servicio Geográfico del Ejército
Dario Gazapo, 8
28024 Madrid, Spain
00 34 91 7115043   00 34 91 7115033

Menorca Tour & Trail Super-Durable Map 1: 40,000 Scale by David & Ros Brawn (Pub. Discovery Walking Guides Ltd. 2005) £7.99/€11.50
ISBN: 1-904946-03-8
Up to date, highly detailed, clear, tough, tear-proof and waterproof - this is the map created by walkers for walkers. Indispensable.

Menorca (Pub. Consell Insular de Menorca, Institut Balear de Turisme)
Free
Basic give-away map distributed in tourist offices, showing main roads, historic sights and beaches, and street plans of the centres of Maó and Ciutadella.

There are plenty of cheap maps around in Menorca's shops. Some are inaccurate and poorly printed, and many are out of date, although there are one or two of interest if you want to know more about archaeological sites.

WALKING BOOKS & INFORMATION

Menorca is not well served with walking guide books, or information, considering how many people go walking on the island. Much of the walking on Menorca is on privately owned land and how writers have dealt with this situation has determined two styles of books; those (like ourselves) who cross uncontested (and unoccupied) private land where public access points exist; and those who insist on trying to cross privately occupied land even when barriers to public access have been erected.

The Uncontested Approach

 **Walk! Menorca** David & Ros Brawn (Pub. Discovery Walking Guides 2005)
144 pages covering 40 fully detailed walking routes complete with 1:40,000 scale colour map sections and GPS waypoints. On completion of our final research in October 2004, all routes were directly accessible on foot.

Walks Around series of little pocket books Distributed by the authors around the resort shops.
These little booklets are just the sort of thing we like to find on sale, encouraging tourists to explore the island at little cost. Being cheap to produce, we would expect these booklets to reasonably up to date but, for example, in the **Walks Around Santa Galdana** title, they say that the *Camí Reial* is blocked just beyond the cave, when this route (Walk 31) has been open for at least two years.

Walk No. 30 - Open All Hours. Free.
A single sheet sketch map available from the golf shop on **Club Son Parc** for a route around **Son Parc**, **Coves Noves** and **Arenal**.

The Contested Approach

Early writers such as Dodo Mackenzie and Rodney Ansell have included routes which cover private ground, and many of these routes have since been closed by owners who are understandably angry at having all and sundry crossing their land as though it was a public right of way. This has lead to confrontations and owners installing ever higher gates and removing access points.

30 Coast & Country Walks around Menorca Dodo Mackenzie (Pub. Gold Son Saura S.A.) €10
Dodo Mackenzie pioneered plenty of walking across Menorca, but unfortunately a lot of it was over private ground resulting in route closures by the owners. Even on uncontested routes such as **Cales Coves**, Dodo's route has fallen into disuse to the point where it has become overgrown and impassable; Dodo refers to her path as the only way in and out of **Cales Coves**, but see our Walk 29 for two more paths and a dirt track.

Landscapes of Menorca Rodney Ansell (Sunflower Books) £9.99 3rd edition 2001
136 pages plus pull-out map. One of the infamous 'blue book' series and

unfortunately suffering from route closures and modifications to the extent that the updates (available on the internet) now run to four A4 pages. Where routes have been closed by the owner then advice given in the updates such as for Walk 14 "There is a gate which is usually locked. The wall beside it is covered with brambles and cannot be climbed. The gate can be climbed if you have reasonably long legs and if you have got this far you should be agile enough. The way to do it is to use the hinge on the left as a foothold, but it is quite high, hence the need for longish legs." Following instructions to deliberately trespass on private land is going to lead you into trouble, and simply shows how urgently this Landscapes title needs a complete rewrite.

CYCLING

Menorca en Velo (Menorca by Bike) by Llorenç Sastre ((Pub. Consell Insular de Menorca, Grup Balear d'Ornitologia i Defensa de la Naturalesa)
This booklet, produced under the auspices of the island government, has no ISBN and can only be found on the island. It contains 20 biking routes, some of which could be used by walkers, although the text is in Menorquín which you might just about decipher if you know some Spanish.

BACKGROUND & REFERENCE BOOKS

The Rough Guide to Mallorca and Menorca by Phil Lee (Pub. Rough Guides 2004) £10.99
ISBN: 1-843532-52-2
Useful, detailed background information as you would expect from Rough Guides, but why lump two very different destinations together in one book?

The Rough Guide to Menorca (Miniguides Series) by Phil Lee (Pub. Rough Guides 2001) £5.99
ISBN: 1-858287-08-1
Light to pack and carry, but getting out of date.

Berlitz Menorca Pocket Guide by Pam Barrett (Pub. Berlitz Publishing Company Ltd. 2004) £4.99
ISBN: 9-812463-96-8
This general guide is small and light - but the downside is a lack of depth and detail.

Birdwatching Guide to Menorca, Ibiza and Formentera by Graham Hearl, Heart, J. Busby (Illustrator) (Pub. Arlequin Publications 1996) £8.95
ISBN: 1-900159-20-1

**The Birds of Menorca** by Enric Ramos (Pub. Editorial Moll 2000) £7.99
ISBN: 8-427307-61-6

**Conquests and Reconquests of Menorca** by Micaela Mata (Pub. M. Mata 1984)
ISBN: 8-439813-87-2
Difficult to find in this English translation, but try amazon.co.uk for a second-hand copy.

**Birds of the Balearic Islands** Muddeman, Hearl & Busby (A&C Black) £27.00
ISBN 0-713665-33-5

**Plants of the Balearic Islands** Anthony Bonner (Moll)
ISBN 8-427304-23-4

**Field Guide to Wild Flowers of Southern Europe** by Paul Davies and Bob Gibbons (Pub. Crowood Press Ltd. 1993) £10.99
ISBN 1-852236-59-0

**Let's Go To The Beach** leaflet (Pub. Consell Insular de Menorca, Grup Balear d'Ornitologia i Defensa de la Naturalesa) Free
Modest little leaflet to pick up from tourist offices, but useful sketch map showing beaches and Z.E.P.A. areas of special protection for birds.

**Archaeological Guide to Minorca** (Pub. Consell Insular de Menorca, Institut Balear de Turisme) Free
Useful explanation of the main historical sites, photos and basic maps. From tourist offices.

WEBSITES

> **www.visitbalears.com** (official Balearic Government Tourist Information)
> **www.cime.es** (Menorca Island Council's site)
> **www.ultimateguide-menorca.com**
> **www.menorca-net.co.uk**
> **www.cntraveller.com/Guides/Spain/Menorca/**
> **www.balearics.com**
> **www.europeforvisitors.com/menorca/**
> **www.red2000.com/spain/baleares/menorca/**
> **www.islandwalking.com/menorca.html**
> **www.menorca-info.com/**

Emergencies (equivalent to the UK's 999 service) Tel. 112

 Taxis

The tourist information office in the airport arrivals hall has an up to date price list for all the resorts and towns.

Maó Plaza Esplanada	971 36 12 83	
Maó Plaza España	971 36 28 91	Radio Taxi 971 36 71 11
Ciutadella, Avda. Constitucion	971 38 11 97	
Alaior (Radio Taxi)	971 36 71 11	
Es Mercadal	971 37 50 27	
Ferreries	971 37 34 84	
Es Migjorn Gran	971 37 00 71 / 971 37 01 05	
San Lluís	971 15 40 83	
Es Castell	971 36 27 79	

The main Tourist Information Offices are in **Maó** and **Ciutadella** (see street plans accompanying Walks 1 & 2 for locations), and there is also an office at the airport. While other resorts may have an office, these are subject to seasonal opening hours.

MARKETS

(usually held mornings only)

Maó	Tuesday and Saturday
Ferreries	Tuesday and Friday
Ciutadella	Friday and Saturday
Es Castell	Monday and Wednesday
Alaior	Thursday

WALKING HOLIDAYS

A number of organisations offer walking package holidays to Menorca; an internet search will pull up half a dozen that specialise in walking overseas.

At the time of research (October 2004), a new venture, Menorca Walking Holidays,(Freephone from within the UK 0800 0724832) was about to be launched by John and Carole Devine, who live on the island. Take a look at their website:
www.menorcawalkingholidays.com

Two bus companies provide public services; TMSA in the centre, south and east, and Torres in the west. Please note:

- these times are for guidance only - do pick up current information from local newspapers, or from tourist or bus offices on arrival,
- services are likely to be less frequent off-season (October-April),
- most major bus stops carry a current timetable,

| * | no Saturday service |
| ** | no service on Sundays or fiestas |

TMSA ROUTES (Note - these buses do not have numbers)

MAÓ - ALAIOR - ES MERCADAL - FERRERIES - CIUTADELLA
Monday to Friday
07.15, 08.15, 09.15, 10.15, 11.15, 12.15, 13.15, 14.15, 15.15, 16.15, 17.15, 18.15, 19.15, 20.15, 21.15, 22.15
Saturday
08.00, 10.00, 11.30, 13.00, 16.00, 18.00, 20.00
Sunday
08.00, 10.00, 11.30, 13.00, 16.30, 19.00 08.00,

CIUTADELLA - FERRERIES - ES MERCADAL - ALAIOR - MAÓ
Monday to Friday
06.45, 07.45, 08.45, 09.45, 10.45, 11.45, 12.45, 13.45, 14.45, 15.45, 16.45, 17.45, 18.45, 19.45, 29.45, 21.45
Saturday
08.00, 10.00, 11.30, 14.30, 16.00, 18.00, 20.00
Sunday
10.00, 11.30, 14.30, 16.30, 19.00

MAÓ - FERRERIES - CALA GALDANA
Monday to Friday
09.15, 14.15, 16.15, 18.15

CIUTADELLA - FERRERIES - CALA GALDANA
Monday to Friday
11.45, 14.45, 8.45

FERRERIES - CALA GALDANA
08.30, 09.45, 10.15, 12.00, 13.45, 15.15, 17.15, 18.15, 19.15

CALA GALDANA - FERRERIES
08.45, 10.00, 10.30, 12.15, 14.00, 15.00, 16.00, 17.30, 18.30, 19.30

CALA GALDANA - CIUTADELLA
09.15, 10.30, 14.00, 16.00

CIUTADELLA - CALA GALDANA
08.45, 10.00, 14.30, 16.55

CALA GALDANA - MAÓ **
10.00

MAÓ - CALA GALDANA **
11.15

MAÓ - ES MIGJORN - SANT TOMÁS **
08.15, 11.15, 14.15, 18.30*

SANT TOMÁS - ES MIGJORN - MAÓ **
09.15, 12.00, 15.00, 19.15*

CIUTADELLA - ES MIGJORN - SANT TOMÁS**
08.15, 14.15, 18.30*

SANT TOMÁS - ES MIGJORN - CIUTADELLA**
09.15, 12.00, 15.00, 19.15*

MAÓ - ALAIOR - TORRE SOLI NOU - SANT JAUME - SON BOU **
08.30, 09.45, 12.45, 14.00, 15.25, 17.00, 19.00

SON BOU - SANT JAUME - TORRE SOLI NOU - ALAIOR - MAÓ **
09.15, 10.30, 11.00, 13.30, 16.30, 17.15, 18.00, 19.35

SON BOU - ALAIOR
09.15, 10.00, 11.00, 16.00, 17.00

ALAIOR - SON BOU
09.45, 10.45, 16.40, 17.40

MAÓ - SANT LLUÍS
08.10**, 08.30, 09.30, 10.30, 11.30, 12.30, 13.30 15.30, 16.30, 17.30, 18.30, 19.30, 20.15

SANT LLUÍS - MAÓ
07.30**, 08.20, 09.10, 10.10, 11.10, 12.10, 13.10, 15.20, 16.10, 17.10, 18.10, 19.10, 20.00

MAÓ - ES CASTELL
07.20**, 07.45**, 08.15**. 08.45**, 09.15,
09.45, 10.15, 10.45, 11.45, 12.15, 12.45, 13.15,
13.45, 14.15 **, 14.45**, 15.15**, 15.45, 14.30**,
16.15, 16.45, 17.45, 18.15, 18.45, 19.15, 19.45,
20.15, 20,45

ES CASTELL - MAÓ
07.30**, 08.00**, 09.00 **, 09.30, 10.00,
10.30, 11.00, 12.00, 12.30, 13.00, 13.30, 14.00,
15.00**, 15.30**, 16.00, 16.30, 17.00, 18.00
18.30, 19.00, 19.30, 20.00, 20.30, 21.00

MAÓ - ALCALFAR
08.30, 09.30, 12.30, 13.30, 15.30, 18.30

ALCALFAR - MAÓ
08.45, 09.45, 12.45, 13.45, 15.45, 18.45

S'ALGAR - MAÓ
09.00, 10.00, 13.00, 14.00, 16.00, 19.00

LAS PALMERAS - MAÓ
08.55, 09.55, 12.55, 13.55, 15.55, 18.55

MAÓ - PUNTA PRIMA
08.30**, 09.30, 10.30, 1.30, 12.30,
13.30, 16.30, 18.30, 19.30

PUNTA PRIMA - MAÓ
09.00**, 10.00, 11.00, 12.00, 13.00,
14.00, 17.00, 19.00, 20.00

MAÓ - BINIBECA
10.30, 14.20, 17.30

BINIBECA - MAÓ
11.00, 14.35, 18.00

SANT CLIMENT - CALA'N PORTER
08.00, 08.45, 09.30, 10.30, 11.45, 12.30,
13.30, 16.00, 17.00, 18.00, 19.00, 19.30

CALA'N PORTER - CANUTELLS
09.30, 10.30, 11.45, 13.30, 16.00, 18.00, 19.30

CALA'N PORTER - MAÓ
10.00, 11.00, 12.15, 13.45, 16.30, 18.30, 20.00

CANUTELLS - MAÓ
09.00, 12.45, 17.15, 19.15

MAÓ - SANT CLIMENT (Sundays only)
09.15, 12.15, 15.15, 18.15

SANT CLIMENT - MAÓ (Sundays only)
09.25, 12.25, 15.25, 18.25

TORRES ROUTES

Nº1 CIUTADELLA - CALA EN BLANES - LOS DELFINES - CALA EN FORCAT
07.15**, 08.15**, 08.45, 09.15, 09.45, 10.15**, 10.45, 11.15**, 12.00, 12.45**, 13.15, 13.45**, 14.15,
14.45**, 15.15, 16.00, 16.45**, 17.30, 18.00**, 18.30, 19.00**, 19.45, 20.30**, 21.15, 21.45**

CALA EN FORCAT - LOS DELFINES - CALA EN BLANES - CIUTADELLA
07.25**, 08.25**, 8.55, 9.25, 9.55, 10.25**, 10.55, 11.25**, 12.10, 12.55**, 13.25, 13.55**, 14.25,
14.55**, 15.25, 16.10, 16.55**, 17.40, 18.10**, 18.40, 19.10**, 19.55, 20.40**, 21.25, 21.55**

Nº2 CIUTADELLA - CALETA - SANTANDRIA - CALA BLANCA
07.00, 08.00, 08.40**, 09.10, 09.40**, 10.10, 10.40**, 11.10, 12.10, 12.40**, 13.10, 13.40**, 14.10,
14.40**, 15.40, 16.40**, 17.40, 18.40, 19.40**, 20.40

CALA BLANCA - SANTANDRIA - CALETA - CIUTADELLA
07.30, 08.30, 08.50**, 09.20, 09.50 **, 10.20, 10.50**, 11.20, 12.20, 12.50**, 13.20, 13.50**, 14.20,
14.50**, 15.50, 16.50**, 17.50, 18.50, 19.50**, 20.50

Nº4 CIUTADELLA - CALETA - CALA'N BOSCH - SON XORIGUER
07.00, 08.00, 08.45**, 09.00, 09.15**, 09.30, 09.45**, 10.00, 10.15**, 10.30, 10.45**, 11.00, 11.30**,
12.00, 12.30**, 12.45**, 13.00, 13.15**, 13.30, 13.45**, 14.00, 14.15**, 14.30, 15.00**, 15.30, 16.00**,
16.30, 17.00**, 17.45, 18.15**, 18.45, 19.15, 20.00, 20.45**, 21.15

SON XORIGUER - CALA'N BOSCH - CALETA - CIUTADELLA
07.10, 08.10, 08.55**, 09.10, 09.25**, 09.40, 09.55**, 10.10, 10.25**, 10.40, 10.55**, 11.10, 11.40**,
12.10, 12.40**, 12.55**, 13.10, 13.25**, 13.40, 13.55**, 14.10, 14.25**, 14.40, 15.10**, 15.40, 16.10**,
16.40, 17.10**, 17.55. 18.25**, 18.55, 19.25, 20.10, 20.55**, 21.25

CIUTADELLA - CALA'N BOSCH (direct service)
10.20

CALA'N BOSCH - CIUTADELLA (direct service)
16.10

Please note that the spelling of Menorcan place names on signs and maps may be spelled in Catalán or Menorquin, and there are also regional variations.

DISCOVERY WALKING GUIDES LTD. TITLES LIST

GPS

GPS The Easy Way
Manual £4.99
Personal Navigator Files - CD
(Oziexplorer format) **Version 2.01** £7.99

SPANISH MAINLAND

Sierra de Aracena - a Walk! Guidebook
Guidebook £11.99
Sierra de Aracena
Tour & Trail Map £2.99
34 Alpujarras Walks
Guidebook £9.99
Alpujarras Super-Durable
Tour & Trail Map £7.99

CANARY ISLANDS

Walk! Lanzarote
Guidebook £11.99
Lanzarote Super-Durable
Tour & Trail Map £7.99
Lanzarote Indestructible Map £4.99
Lanzarote Plant&Flower Guide £2

Walk! La Gomera (2nd edition)
Guidebook £11.99
La Gomera Super-Durable
Tour &Trail Map £7.99
Drive! La Gomera
Touring Map £2.50
La Gomera Plant&Flower Guide £2

35 Tenerife Walks
Guidebook £9.99
Walk! Tenerife South
Guidebook £5.99
Tenerife Super-Durable
Walkers' Maps £4.99
Tenerife Paper Edition
Walkers' Maps £2.99
Tenerife Indestructible Map £4.99

Drive! Tenerife Touring Map £2.50

Tenerife Plant&Flower Guide £2

Gran Canaria Mountains
Tour & Trail Map £5
Gran Canaria Plant&Flower Guide £2

Walk! La Palma
Guidebook £11.99
La Palma Super-Durable
Tour & Trail Map £7.99

BALEARIC ISLANDS

Walk! Mallorca (North & Mountains)
Guidebook £11.99
Mallorca North & Mountains Super-Durable
Tour & Trail Map £7.99
Walk! Mallorca West
Guidebook £11.99
Mallorca West Super-Durable
Tour & Trail Map £7.99
Walk! Menorca
Guidebook £11.99
Menorca Super-Durable
Tour & Trail Map £7.99

PORTUGAL, INCLUDING MADEIRA

Madeira Super-Durable
Tour & Trail Map £7.99
35 Madeira Walks
Guidebook £9.99

Algarve - Loule
Walking Guide £5
Algarve - Silves
Walking Guide £5

MALTA & GOZO

Malta & Gozo Walking Guides £5

ANDORRA

Walk! Andorra
Guidebook £11.99
Andorra Super-Durable
Tour & Trail Map £7.99

HOW TO GET HOLD OF OUR PUBLICATIONS

To order direct from us by mail order, use the form below, or write to us at the address below.

If you are ordering direct from us, please:
- complete your details in BLOCK CAPITALS
- write the full title(s) of the publications you require
- enclose your payment (please note that post & packing is free)
- make your cheque payable to:

Discovery Walking Guides Ltd.
and post to:
Discovery Walking Guides Ltd.
10 Tennyson Close
Northampton NN5 7HJ

TITLE(S) ORDERED	ITEM COST

I enclose my cheque for this TOTAL
(free post & packing)

YOUR NAME

ADDRESS

POST CODE

*TEL N°

**email   @

* for order enquiries only   ** for enewsletters and updates

Spending a lot of our time amongst dramatic landscapes, we appreciate the value of an accurately researched and well written walk description. Abroad, in a foreign land, is no place to find yourself lost and in danger. Knowing this, we operate a 'no compromise' policy to all of DWG's walking routes. We walk every route - repeatedly if necessary - to make sure that we have an accurate walk description. Then we try to write a detailed walk description in an inspirational tone so that you know how we felt on that route. We've slogged up that impossible looking ascent, marvelled at those panoramas, found paths through apparently pathless wilderness, have gratefully arrived at our destination. It's not always fun, but it has always been an adventure. Our GPS ground survey system means that we know exactly where we've been, except when there is poor GPS reception and we tell you this.

This 'no compromise'policy is much appreciated by users of DWG walking guides, as our post bag testifies. This means that with a DWG guidebook, you can confidently embark on the adventures it contains, knowing that we've researched every route to the highest standard.

We still marvel at every "Your guide made my holiday"letter we receive, just as we did at the first one we ever received. Bringing adventure and enjoyment to people is very pleasing, and we are very good listeners to what our readers would like to appear in a walk description.

In **Walk! Menorca** you'll find:-
- Walking route summary including Effort, Time, Distance, Ascents/Descents, and Refreshments
- Frequent timings so that you can judge your progress against ours
- Fully detailed walk description
- Detailed map for every walking route
- GPS Waypoints (grid references) for every key point on the route
- Full GPS Waypoint lists for all walking routes
- National and regional Locator Maps
- lots of useful background information

We haven't done all this just because **Walk! Menorca** is special, which it certainly is; this is our normal 'no compromise' approach to giving you everything you need in a walking guide book. Now, go out there and enjoy it, safe in the knowledge that we have been there before and we have a full GPS track and waypoint record of where we've been. Generally our routes are straightforward, so long as you follow the walk descriptions; some routes do have some potentially confusing junctions. While many of our routes are linear, we have grouped them together matrix fashion, when possible, so that you can easily combine routes. All that is necessary is for you to be there, marvelling at the beautiful landscapes, historical and archaeological sites, the amazing flora and fauna, plus masses of new discoveries.

David & Ros Brawn
Directors of Discovery Walking Guides Ltd
(That's us in some of the Walk photographs)

Menorca

Tour & Trail

1:40,000 Scale Map

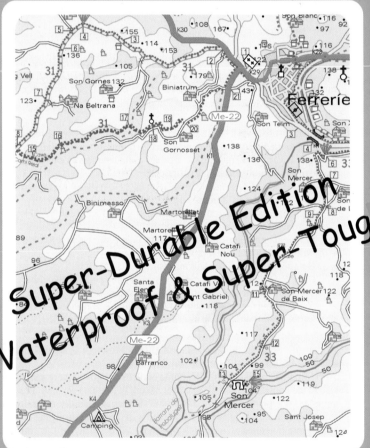

Fully Updated 3rd Editio
on Super-Durable polyme
£7.99 UK / €11.50 Menorc